Copyrighted Material

"Art of Team Building: Essential Strategies for Building Your Dream Team & Improving Team Performance"

All Rights Reserved

Copyright 2019. Mekhal Aly

No part of this book may be reproduced or transmitted I any form or by any means, graphic, electronic, or mechanical, including photocopying, recording, taping, or by any information storage retrieval system, without the permission in writing from the author or publisher.

Table of Contents

Chapter 1: Welcome and Introduction

Chapter 2: What Is Meant by Team Building?

Chapter 3: What is a Well-Built Team?

Chapter 4: How to Build Your Team?

Chapter 5: Different Types of Teams You Should Know About

Chapter 6: Selecting Your Team!

Chapter 7: How to Lead Your Team!

Chapter 8: The Importance of Communication

Chapter 9: The Importance of Trust

Chapter 10: The Importance of Team Culture

Chapter 11: The Importance of Setting Team Rules

Chapter 12: Benefits of Team Building Exercises

Chapter 13: Evolving Your Team & The Future

Chapter 14: Tips for Managing Team Stress

Chapter 15: Team Building Issues

Chapter 16: Thank You!

Chapter 1: Welcome and Introduction

Hello, everyone!

I welcome you all to my book on team building and ensuring that team operates at optimum levels.

Did you know that around 85% of failures occurring in the workplace can be traced back to poor teamwork?

Well, now you know!

Having an efficient team is something which can't be stressed enough if you wish any business to grow.

Teams having low levels of engagement aren't able to meet their revenue and productivity goals, and we don't want that, right?

Almost every executive, and I'm talking more near 99% here, believe inefficient teamwork has a negative impact on a project's result.

Furthermore, employees who have lower team engagement are more likely to leave organizations. And trying to find replacements for certain team members who have left, especially when you have a deadline nearing, isn't an easy task.

And even when everyone knows the importance of team building and management, not a lot of companies spend the resources to increase teamwork and to create a cooperative environment… It is either that or companies don't know how to effectively go about it all.

Organizations need to ask themselves, are they doing everything possible to build, support, and lead more effective teams?

What is the use of a team if doesn't work well, right?

Effective teams are everywhere around us.

Successful business like Starbucks, Amazon, Apple, Microsoft, and more (whether you agree with how they operate or not) are nothing without an efficient team building and monitoring model.

The same holds true for the other sectors we see, with every individual serving a specifically vital part while working seamlessly with others to produce the desired results.

I have already created an entire course on Project Management (as well as published a book about it), which also includes forming teams for a project and the proven ways to monitor progress.

So, if you want to check all of that content out, I will greatly appreciate it.

However, in this book, I will be focusing more on the Team Building aspect, how to select team members, how to monitor team progress, how to keep team morale high, tips for better team communication, and a whole lot more!

I have tried to offer all of the information in the easiest manner possible.

I hope you give this book a read and I'm able to convey information you will be able to use in the real world.

As for what you will learn from this book, I have done my best to help you cover not only the basics of what is meant by team building, but other practices as well which can help maintain effective teams for the long run.

Among many other benefits, effective teams can:

- Produce positive results
- Encourage creativity
- Encourage engagement
- Establish and maintain strong relationships
- Establish and maintain strong communication
- Boost productivity

You can't deny it...

Proper Team building is one of the most important investments you can make for both your organization and the people within it.

You might be wondering; how exactly can you build more effective teams?

The answers to all such questions will be given in this book!

So, let's begin!

Chapter 2: What Is Meant by Team Building?

In this chapter, I'll begin by talking about what is meant by team building.

If you do your research, you will get to know about a number of experts who have talked about ways to build effective teams. From Bill Gates to Jeff Bezos, there are many examples you can learn from.

The important thing to take note of is even though you have assembled a team, it doesn't mean you will be able to get the result you desire.

Even the great teams can't be the mightiest teams out there without understanding what is meant by teamwork or by complementing each other's skills and talents.

Every team member might be super skilled on their own, however, it won't matter much if they aren't able to come together as a team.

Poor communication and lack of collaboration serve as downfalls of teams that might seem perfect on paper.

When you bring people together to accomplish collective goals they need to talk to each other and they need to do so with respect and empathy as well as efficiency.

Have you ever been in a situation where a company ends up prioritizing personality over skill? A list of potentials candidates might have similar skills and experience, but in the end, the ones with likable personalities are hired?

Well, this is because, we, as humans, have found out that people with good personalities are naturally easier to get along with. They are easy to communicate with and they also exude more empathy.

A person might be a master at a craft, but organizations won't hire them if they have a personality which is closed off and not ready to work with others on a team.

No one has time for such drama especially when there are important projects to be completed.

Team members end up working for months or even years with one another. They might even be spending more time with each other than their friends or family. Getting along with one another, at least, on a professional level, is key to efficient team building.

Team building isn't easy, but it is doable!

In this book I will address many of the best practices which lead to the formation of successful
teams and how to build your own.

We'll talk about evaluating your own team before making changes. Leading a team effectively whether that team is in your office, virtual or remote. We will cover how to get your team to communicate effectively with each other. How to improve trust and build a positive culture in the work environment. The challenges you will face while building a team, for example, geographical barriers, language barriers, and more.

There are also team building exercise which can help improve communication as well as build respect while allowing team members to have fun.

Another aspect of team building is knowing when and how to evolve with time. I will be going over that as well. Also, managing stress is important, too. You can't have an effective team if the members are stressed out.

By the end of this book, I hope I to have provided you with enough useful information for you to apply certain techniques and best practices immediately to your own team.

So, you can see that when we talk about team building, we have to take into consideration a number of features.

But don't worry, I will be with you every step of the way as we go over everything there is to know about building and maintaining effective teams.

Chapter 3: What is a Well-Built Team?

When we talk about what is a well-built team, we are talking about the attributes of well-built teams.

"Coming together is a beginning. Keeping together is progress. Working together is success."- Henry Ford

Take note that influential team development is the road to a successful team.

Various models have been proposed by certain experts for the development of a team. So, it is a good idea to know about these models. When followed, these models can help generate an increased revenue for any company while ensuring the said team continues to work on efficient levels.

One of such models was proposed by an educational psychologist by the name Bruce Tuckman.

Let's see what he had to say.

He identified a five stage model which could assist in the development of highly effective teams.

The five stages are Forming, Storming, Norming, Performing and Adjourning.

Breaking these down (just a bit):

Forming

In this stage of the model, most team members are positive and polite. Of course, some are anxious because they haven't fully understood what work the team is supposed to do. Others members are simply excited about the task ahead.

As team leader, you have to play a dominant role at this stage. Why? It is because the roles and responsibilities of team members aren't clear yet.

Do keep in mind this stage can last for some time, as team members begin to work together, and as they put in the effort to get to know their new colleagues.

Storming

Then we have the Storming stage. This is where team members start to push against the boundaries which were established in the forming stage. And yes, Storming is the stage where many teams do tend to fail.

How does it start, though?

It often begins when there is a conflict between the natural working styles of team members. I mean, people have different working styles. And that's all well and good unless these styles start to clash and cause unforeseen problems. A frustrated team isn't a good team.

Also, Storming can occur when team members begin to challenge your authority or they begin to take over someone else's role because specific roles haven't been made clear. Other instances include feeling overwhelmed by the workload or not being sure about their responsibilities.

Norming

With time, the team moves into the norming stage. This is when team members start to resolve their differences. You will notice team members appreciating what everyone brings to the table. They will respect your authority as the leader.

Due to better knowing each other, team members are open to socializing in a respectable manner. They are also less hesitant to ask each other for help or feedback. They also feel more committed to the goals of a project.

Now, due to new things being introduced in the project, the normal phase can go back into the storming phase.

Performing

This stage is reached when all of the hard work leads to the achievement of the team's goal. The structures and processes you have set up, as the leader, support this well.

It feels easy to be part of the team at this stage. The good news is people who join or leave the team won't disrupt overall performance.

Adjourning

Many teams will get to reach this stage eventually.

Project teams exist for only a fixed period, and even permanent teams may be disbanded through organizational restructuring, depending on certain circumstances.

Team members who prefer routine, or who have been able to develop close working relationships with colleagues, are likely to find this stage difficult. This is true if their future looks uncertain.

Now, that were are done with that model, let's move on to the certain characteristics an effective and successful team has.

Clear Goals

Looking at successful teams, each member has a clear knowledge of the team's overall aim. You can't expect to reach something if you aren't clear about what you want to achieve.

To be successful, every member has to proactively take part in the achievement of a common goal.

A goal reflects the purpose of the team. You know? Why the team was created in the first place.

By mentioning clear goals, it means the said goals should be attainable, relevant and measurable. Furthermore, the said team must have all the prerequisites to attain such goals.

The leader is responsible for making goals clear and monitoring the progress of team members.

Defined Tasks

For any team to become successful members must know their role in achieving the common goal.

The team leader must assign specific tasks to each member. These tasks are to completed to help teams make progress toward the common goal.

Again, it falls on the leader to ensure proper check and balance. Every team member need to carry their weight and fulfill their duties.

Strong Communication

Every successful team out there has strong communication. Without proper communication, team members feel lost.

Effective and meaningful communication keeps all the team members informed about what needs to be done and how to go about it.

More importantly, communication helps develop trust and honesty throughout the team.

The leader is responsible for arranging team meetings and even individual meetings to make sure communication is going strong. The leader should also make team members feel welcome if they have any feedback or a question to ask.

Decision Making

Many might not realize this, but decision making is a trait which isn't exclusive for leaders. Every team member has to make informed decisions themselves when it comes to how they will achieve their specific goals when working on a project.

Each member has to keep the interests of the team in mind and show care when working with others while making any decision.

Also, the leader, depending on the case, should allow members to make their own decisions. Allowing team members to make such decisions helps enhance confidence and interest in a member's relevant task.

Of course, the leader must discuss various models which should be used for decision making prior to the performing stage.

Fair Participation

At the end of the day, the team members are what make the team successful. Each member is a cog in a machine with each cog having its own role to play to achieve certain goals. Every team member needs to participate in the capacity that is expected of them.

Also, the leader must make sure there isn't an imbalance in work load. Tasks should be distributed equally among members. Again, regular check and balance is essential to ensure everyone is participating in a fair and balanced manner.

Conflict Management

Conflicts are natural to arise in any team. The important thing is to manage them appropriately to create a positive working environment.

Due to every member being an important part of a team, their ideas and suggestions should be welcomed and respected by the team leader. Showing respect can help with managing conflicts if they arise.

Not being able to address certain conflicts on time can lead to lowered productivity and even the team being dispersed.

Positive Working Atmosphere

Having a positive working environment is essential. A comfortable working environment is key when it comes to boosting productivity and engagement. For such an atmosphere to be created, every team member has to play their part.

Team members should be self-aware. Are they being difficult when other team members ask for help? Are they doing the work they are being asked to do?

Alienation should be eliminated if you want to have an effective team.

Appreciating Diversity

As team leader, you need to instill a sense of appreciating diversity in your team. Every member should be open to new suggestions from others and treat each other with respect.

Regardless of their sociocultural backgrounds, team member should be given fair opportunities to take part in achieving goals.

Take note, diversity, if it is managed properly, can lead to impressive success. It is all about allowing people to bring their viewpoints forward and then seeing which can work for the betterment of the team. It also creates a culture of support within the team.

I hope these common attributes found in successful teams help you in creating your own team and encouraging a sense of mutual understanding and respect.

As team leader, if falls on you to lead by example. By making everything clear for your team, you will be able to foster a successful environment.

Chapter 4: How To Build Your Team?

In chapter we're going to cover how to build a team. So, let's begin!

The type of team you build can let you know about the productivity levels your team is going to have and whether or not you will be able to achieve the goals you have set.

From what I can tell, one of the things leaders are thinking about is the performance and relationships of their team.

It all comes down to the team building skills you have.

As a leader, you should be able to build a team which not only bring forward the skills required to get a certain task done, but also members who are able to work together, using specific skills, to amplify overall productivity.

For those wondering how to create a productive and effective team, here are five steps you should know about:

Step 1: Establishing Leadership

Being a leader, in name, isn't enough. You have to establish your leadership when dealing with your team members.

If your employees trust your judgement (as a leader), they will tend to work effectively even when you aren't around.

Of course, this doesn't mean you have to be too authoritative and bossy. That won't work!

What you need to do is establish leadership through open communication and fostering a working environment which is about trust and transparency.

In larger organizations, team managers or leaders can't be everywhere at once. However, if your employees trust your judgements they will work effectively even when you're not around them all the time.

Step 2: Establishing Professional Relationships With Team Members

Having a professional relationship with your team members will make you more capable of understanding their needs and how to help them work with others.

You should learn about your team member's skill sets, what motivates them, what they like to do or don't like, and such. Having such information will aid you in using a member's skills to its fullest potential.

Furthermore, allowing team members to be share their feedback and taking part in the decision making process can also help you form strong professional bonds within in the team.

Step 3: Building Professional Relationships Between Employees

While leader-team member relationship is important, so is the professional relationship between employees. Members should show each other respect and be willing to cooperate with each other to achieve certain goals.

By having strong bonds between team members, you can decrease the chances of conflicts arising. You should encourage members to work together on tasks. You should also encourage bonding time during breaks or even plan group activities.

Step 4: Fostering Teamwork

Giving rise to effective teamwork can't be stressed enough if you wish to build a productive team.

You should encourage your team to share information, both amongst themselves and within the wider organization.

Again, communication is key, and I'm not just talking about having group meetings here.

Opt for group activities that help other team members connect with each other. Have members work as teams where everyone feels free to share their opinions and suggestions pertaining to certain issues.

Build an environment where every member understands not only their importance but the importance of the other people they are working with.

Step 5: Setting Ground Rules

You have to set ground rules!

Your team must understand what they should and shouldn't be doing as well as how to go about performing their individual tasks by following the ground rules which have been set. Having a set of core rules and values offer a guide to everyone.

It is a good idea to involve your team in the rule making process so they don't feel you are forcing them to follow certain things.

So, bringing this chapter to a close, team building is one of the most important responsibilities a manager or leader has.

Take note, it isn't something which can be achieved in a short time. Building a productive team and keeping it productive is an ongoing process. With time you will see your team members becoming more trustful toward one another and more open to working together for the betterment of the organization.

Chapter 5: Different Types Of Teams You Should Know About

When talking about building a team, you have to understand the different types of teams you can opt for depending on the type of projects which need to be worked on.

The different needs of organizations have led to the creation and evolution of different types of team. There are permanent teams and temporary ones. Others are part of the corporate hierarchy, while others are adjunct. It all depends on the need of an organization.

As a leader or team manager, you will likely find yourself working with different types of teams. I have talked about being a project manager in another course I created, if you want to check it out.

Coming to statistical data, about 75% of employers rate teamwork and collaboration as "very important".

Only 18% of employees get communication evaluations at their performance reviews.

39% of surveyed employees believe people in their own companies don't collaborate enough.

Before we go ahead with the most common types of business teams in the workplace, first, let's identify the core difference between teams and groups.

Groups and teams

Business companies tend to include both groups and teams.

Groups are normally formed around common interests or purposes with the goal of sharing information, however, there is no collective accountability. It can be a social club or a workgroup with volunteer efforts.

Teams' focus is collective performance. This is where the team members have both individual and mutual accountabilities. That is why companies create teams to bring together groups of people with the required skills and interests to work toward a common goal for the betterment of an organization.

Of course, each type comes with its set of strengths and weaknesses.

The type of team you need depends on your purposes, location, and organizational structure.

For those who might not know, the early concept of teams rose to popularity back in the 1970s. People were still trying to polish team building back then. Moving on, modern teamwork is fully integrated into the activities and organizational culture.

The main advantage of having a team is that it brings together different individuals with a diverse set of skills and talents. They all come together to accomplish a set goal. It might even be something no one else was able to accomplish before.

Furthermore, communication levels need to be higher on teams. Also, effective teams can discover new approaches and improve product and service quality.

But coming to the reason I created this book, unfortunately, not all teams are able to perform successfully.

When managers or leaders don't care enough about creating and supporting strong teams, it leads to members losing interest in what they are supposed to do. It can result in people leaving the company due to poor communication, not feeling valued, and such.

Teams are unable to work well if they have no defined purposes and the required resources.

"A successful team is a group of many hands and one mind." - Bill Bethel

Project Team

A project team is a group of employees that are supposed to work collectively and have shared goals and strategies.

In this type of team, you need to structure work in a specific, measurable and time-constrained way.

In Project teams, the roles and responsibilities, including deadlines, are clear.

The four subspecies of project teams are:

Functional team

A functional team is a permanent one. Such a team includes members of the same department with different responsibilities. A manager is responsible for everything. Members are supposed to report to the manager.

Take note, a functional team can be usually recognized in traditional project management companies.

Cross-functional team

A cross-functional team is one which consists of members from different departments. This kind of team handles specific tasks requiring different expertise and inputs.

While Cross-functional teams seem to be becoming increasingly popular, some say having too many of such teams isn't a good idea.

Matrix team

In this team you have a 2-boss system. This means an individual has to report to a different manager for their work. A matrix team, as the name implies, is the product of a Matrix management approach.

Such a team helps top managers to retain control over the project without being involved in the decisions which need to be made.

Contract team

A contract team is an outsourced team. As the name states, this is where the team members are tied down by a contract.

All ties to the said team can be easily cut by a client once the project has been completed or a contract has ended.

The role of the manger, in such a team, is to maintain constant communication between the customer and team members, to compensate for the lack of the team's physical presence.

Now, coming back to the main types, we have:

Self-managed teams

Self-managed teams happen to consist of employees of the same company who work together. Although they do have a wide set of objectives, their key goal is to reach a common result.

As the name states, there is no manager here. The members of such teams determine rules and expectations. They solve problems by working together and also and have shared responsibilities.

If you are pondering about having a self-managed team, attention should be paid to the levels of responsibility and the autonomy which is to be given to the team.

The main advantages of having self-managed teams are:

Improved motivation because of autonomy.

Ability to manage own time to handle tasks.

Pride in team accomplishments because of having shared responsibility

Of course, there are some disadvantages you should know about.

One of the weak points about having self-managed teams is the lack of hierarchical authority which can favor personal relationships over good judgment.

Virtual team

A virtual team involves employees who work in different locations. They rely on the power of communication and collaboration tools to get things done which working together.

Such a team is a good way for organizations to hire experts who might be living in some other location.

There are different types of virtual teams. These can be characterized by 3 dimensions which are time, space and culture.

Time is about when people work (for example during different hours, on different shifts, they are in different time-zones).

Space is about where people work (for example if they are right next to each other or perhaps hundreds of kilometers away).

Culture is about how people work (this includes factors such as gender, age, race, economic factors, language, education, nationality, social, religion, etc.)

Operational team

An operational team is about supporting other types of teams. Such a team is formed to make sure all office processes go smoothly.

Problem-solving team

A problem-solving team is usually temporary. As the name states, such a team is focused on solving a specific issue. Such teams are generally created to handle a financial crisis, a big event or challenge. Problem-solving teams are just that, teams for solving specific problems.

So, what's your choice when it comes team building?

If you are hesitant about the kind of team approach to opt for, try to ask yourself at least the following questions:

What are the goals of the potential team?

How many people are required?

How do you identify their roles?

Will their engagement be temporary or permanent?

Do the employees require a strong leader?

Is it necessary to be located in a single place?

For some quick suggestions, if your goal is to perform a project which requires input from marketing, design and customer support departments, it could be a good idea to go for a cross-functional team.

If you are going to outsource designers, an agency or people to work remotely, then a mixture of virtual and contract teams is where it's at.

Take note, if you look around the current business landscape, most (if not all) successful teams are hybrids.

Chapter 6: Selecting Your Team!

The selection process, y'all!

One of the most essential steps to ensure you are building an effective team deals with knowing the right way to go about selecting the said team.

It is all about coming up with the right group of individuals who have what it takes to complete a project.

This can be quite tough especially when you want to build a company from scratch. Due to limitations, you have to carefully plan your strategy and resources.

Take note human resources is a good way to come up with the right team you want to have.

This is because the more capable people you have working for your company, the better your image, reputation, services, etc. will be.

Of course, picking the right professionals to build an effective team for a certain project is more challenging than it might look to some. There is a lot of risk involved. You don't want to waste time and resources creating an ineffective team, right?

So, here are a few tips to help you select the best professionals for your team:

Look for Capable Communicators

Team members should be great communicators for them to be receptive, to understand, and to act on what you tell them to. Such people are the ones who know how to listen, respond, and show respect to the others they are talking to in a business setting.

Well-Organized and Self-Disciplined

You team members should have good organizational skills and self-discipline. Not only should know how to manage their time to handle the tasks they have been given, their self-discipline should be seen in the way they manage their workspace and how they interact with others while on the clock.

Capable Project Manager

The one who leads a team is a reflection of how the team will do. Ask yourself, will you leading the team or will you need to hire someone more capable to handle a project?

Being the manager of a project isn't an easy task. So, do keep that in mind when you contemplate becoming a project manager or bringing someone else to the oversee the team.

Hire Who Fit

When it is time for you to hire people, you have to be 100% objective.

Personal favors and relationships don't always work out in such cases. Ignoring the best candidate to hire a less capable sibling of a friend isn't the right choice to make.

Go over the potential candidate's background (such as experience, skills, and attitude) to see if what they bring to the table can help with completing a project. You should also do some research by going over their social media footprint to see what kind of individual you are hiring.

You can also consider giving them a small test to see if they are the right choice for your team.

Resourceful Individuals

If you want your team to be resourceful, you will need to look for resourceful individuals. If you can, opt for individuals who aren't only capable of handling their tasks (pertaining to the project) but also have connection to different clients, experts, organizations, and such.

Hiring influential people in your team can led to a number of benefits to help your business grow.

Prioritizing Skills and Knowledge

As far as my opinion goes (as well as what other experts say), you should seek skills, knowledge, and experience over certifications.

This means you shouldn't choose solely based on certifications. I say this because by doing so you risk getting unskilled and inexperienced project members who can hinder a project's progress.

Someone might look good on paper, but to have an effective team, you need members who have proof when it comes to how productive they are. They need to have skills and knowledge. Not just the achievement of finishing college or courses.

People Willing to Commit

You need team members you can trust. They should be willing to commit to the work you want them to do. This includes being able to handle risks, setbacks, fear, as well as other negative emotions and situations they might come across.

During the interview, let candidates know what to expect from the role. See how committed or motivated they are to fulfill their duties if made part of the team.

Bringing it all to a close, always be careful when choosing your project team members. You can't have a successful team if you don't make the right decisions when it comes to selecting team members.

Chapter 7: How to Lead Your Team!

Over the years I have seen that the greatest asset when it comes to leading teams and managing projects is not all about certain technical tools and procedures but skillfully relating to people.

As far as my opinion goes, you can have all the processes and procedures about team building and managing memorized, have all the project manager certifications, and be an expert in all related thing, and the list goes on!

But if you are unable to skillfully manage human relationships and interactions, you won't be able to successfully lead teams, let alone manage successful projects.

However, don't be hard on yourself if you think you aren't the greatest leader out there. There are ways you can easily improve your leadership skills.

Also, do keep in mind, it is okay to make mistakes on your leadership journey. We all make mistakes. What's important is to keep working on improving ourselves.

Criticizing People... Don't!

One of the easiest ways to demotivate people is to constantly criticize them or complain about them.

As a leader, you need to do better. If someone on your team makes a mistake, put it in perspective with the things the said team member does well.

When correcting a team member, you shouldn't forget to focus on the positives they bring to the table. Also, give constructive criticism instead of being mean about it.

Offer Praise

Positively reinforcing a desired behavior leads to people becoming more likely to repeat the certain behavior.

When your team members do the right thing and achieve certain milestones, you should praise them.

And yes, the praise and appreciation you give should be honest for it to mean anything.

Encourage Feedback

Team members feel valued when they realize their feedback holds weight. While you are the leader and there are certain things you wish to convey to the team, make time to hear what your team members have to say as well.

Be respectful of the opinions and ideas team members share with you even if you don't agree with them. Also, try to see things from their point of view.

Self-Accountability

Being a leader doesn't mean you can't do any wrong. Your team will appreciate you more as a leader if they know you're someone who accepts their own mistakes.

One of the greatest personality traits you can develop is that of humility.

Don't put the blame of your mistakes on others. Be self-accountable if you wish to become better. Be willing to apologize to those affected by the mistake.

Clear Goals

How can a leader lead when they don't know where to lead the team to?

That is why setting clear goals is essential. Goals are the primary drivers of any team's intensity and persistence.

Assigning team members specific goals results in higher performance than general goals.

Goals aid in organizing and directing attention by necessity. They also encourage strategy and planning.

Opt for the classic SMART Goal framework. SMART stands for Specific, Measurable, Attainable, Results-Oriented, Time-Bound.

Be The Leader You Would Want to Lead You

It is said, treat other how you want to be treated.

The same goes for leadership. Become the kind of leader you want to be led by.

Many people out there wish to become leaders due to the power, prestige, money and other things they will acquire. Not many of them focus on becoming good leaders.

Great leadership isn't about bossing people around. It is about inspiring and guiding people towards a common goal for everyone's benefit.

As a leader you should work to build your team up. You should give them credit for their work. As mentioned, you should praise their efforts and reward them when they succeed.

Becoming a good leader will take time. But if you keep at it, you are sure to become one and lead a successful team.

Chapter 8: The Importance of Communication

With you having read this book, you must have noticed I have mentioned communication quite a number of times throughout.
Your team need effective communication not just between the members but with you as well.

Frequent communication is essential. This type of communication means to keep everyone in the loop both in person and via technology.

As a leader or manager, you should care about how to keep team members stay informed through regular communication.

It is becoming important for team members to clearly know what their fellow team members are up to. This includes their ideas and their plans or strategies for carrying a project forward.

Any communication breakdown can take quite a toll on the overall workload. It can cause more challenges for you and your team to face.

Furthermore, through communication, you can give rise to trust and cooperation within the team which are attributed effective teams have.

Now, how does one communicate with the team more effectively?

Let me give you an answer to that question. Here's an entire list!

One-on-One Interactions

Successful teams can't be created if you don't have team members who are purposeful in their interactions.

One-on-one interactions are essential not only when it comes time for you to hire someone but also when they have become part of a team.

During the hiring process, you should set your expectations and needs. Tell a potential candidate about what the project's demands, the norms of your company for employees to follow, and such.

After they become part of the team, instead of always having team meetings, opt for one-on-one meetings with the team members to help make them feel valued as well as to listen to what they have to say.

Two-way Feedback

For you to have good communication within the workplace, you need to encourage two-way feedback.

In a workplace, feedback is essential to generate results that can help grow a company by moving toward certain goals.

Take note, a common mistake certain leaders make when offering their feedback is turning the entire thing into a one-way dialogue. They tend to offer no opportunity to team members to bring forth their comments and concerns.

In contrast, encouraging two-way feedback is a sign of good communication in professional settings.

Make sure the team members don't feel hesitant to come forward with their suggestions.

Team Building Activities

Team building activities, even if you aren't a fan of them yet, are a great way to positively impact productivity and overall teamwork.

Such activities can aid in boosting communication between team members. It is also the recommended way to foster professional relationships within a team.

You should opt for creating opportunities for members of your team to collaborate through activities. These can include a team lunch, certain ice breaker games during meetings, puzzle solving games or even an outdoor activity.

It is recommended you try and plan group activities at least twice a month to help everyone come together for better communication.

Appropriate Platforms For Communication

Don't hesitate to go digital to improve communication.

According to the needs of your project, certain communication tools can be an effective way for the whole team to meet up.

With effective task management software, you can help streamline communication between team members. Through such a platform, they can exchange messages relevant to their tasks.

There could be a group chat created by team members where they can share certain images or videos they might have felt were funny to lighten the mood.

Making use of task management software helps do away with lengthy email chains and the frustration that comes with miscommunication.

Having a record of what a member said can help others know about the overall progress and what they are supposed to do.

Chapter 9: The Importance Of Trust

Your team is going to have very different personalities in it, and knowing how to manage all of them is going to be your job as team leader.

However, have you ever had the chance to manage people who didn't trust one another?

Let me tell you right now, the entire ordeal is very challenging!

A team without trust isn't a team!

In fact, it can be defined as a group of individuals who are simply working together, or trying to, without any actual progress.

Not having trust can lead to many issues including not sharing information, arguing about rights and responsibilities, not willing to cooperate, and more!

Regardless of how talented these individuals may be, if they don't trust each other, the team isn't getting anywhere.

With trust in place, each member of the team becomes stronger due to realizing they are part of a group. They know they support each other as everyone plays a part in reaching certain goals.

So, when building a team, you need to focus on trust.

And how can you build trust in a team?

You need to understand what is meant by trust. According to a definition, trust is a "reliance on the character, ability, strength, or truth of someone or something."

Going with such a definition, trust means you rely on someone else to do the right thing. This is because you believe in the said person's integrity and strength. The belief is so strong you are able to put yourself on the line.

Trust within a team is essential because it offers a sense of safety and support. When team members feel safe and supported, they are likely to open up, communicate better, take appropriate risks, and such.

With there being no trust, you will be dealing with less innovation, collaboration, creative thinking, and team productivity.

Trust also helps team members to share knowledge for the betterment of the team.

Let's go over how you, as the leader or manager, can foster a culture of trust within your team.

Lead by Example

For your team to have trust, you will need to lead by example. By showing team members you trust others, they are more likely to follow suit and do the same.

Communicate Openly

Being open in the way you communicate is also essential for building trust. Be honest with your team members. Letting them know they are valued will enable them to open up and communicate better.

Opting for team building activities can also help with open communication and building trust.

Personal Bond

By seeing each other as people, teams can foster a trusting relationship within itself.

Again, coming to leading by example, share some personal stories with your team members and encourage them to do the same (without invading anyone's privacy). This will help everyone get to know each other better even if it just learning about each other's hobbies, likes, passions, interests, and such.

Don't Be Quick to Blame

When working on a project, mistakes are bound to happen. And yes, it can be very easy to put the blame on someone because everyone is pointing fingers. Doing so can weaken the trust in a team and sour the overall environment.

Instead of being quick to place the blame, encourage everyone in the team to think about the mistake in a constructive way.

What can be done to fix the issue and move forward as a team? What can be done to ensure such an issue doesn't occur again?

As a leader, there will be times you might have to step up and shoulder the blame yourself. Doing so will show the entire team you aren't the type of leader who is willing to throw everyone under the bus. Such are the leaders who build trust within teams.

The Cliques

Having certain people strike a stronger bond with each while working in a team is natural. Certain teams might have smaller team within a team depending on the friendships that form. While that is all well and good, having such cliques can be an issue if it is negatively impacting other members.

Due to cliques, some individuals might feel isolated. There might also be trust issues between two or more cliques.

As a leader, you should discourage negative cliques and remind everyone how they are part of a whole and the importance of working together.

Also, if you feel some team members are unwilling to come forward, you can try to address the issue by making the process anonymous.

Building Trust Virtually

Building trust is also essential when working with a virtual team. I say this because you might end up handling a team where a group of people have never met face to face, or who have never spoken to one another personally.

It might sound daunting, but trust can be built between people living miles apart.

You can schedule a virtual "meet and greet" if it's a new team. This will help everyone get to know one another as individuals.

You can also create a web page for your team's project, and then ask team members to write a paragraph or two about their personal history and interests.

Furthermore, you should also make sure everyone on the team is aware of other member's expertise and skills. They should also realize the value each individual contributes to the group as a whole.

Encouraging team members to treat each other just as they would if they were working face to face is important. By this I mean team members should make every effort to be on time for conference calls or web meetings.

With virtual teams, as team leader, you will need to amp your communication. Due to them not seeing you face-to-face, your word holds a lot of value. So, ensure you keep your professional promises and are available when needed to address issues.

Chapter 10: The Importance of Team Culture

We have to talk about Team Culture.

In many projects, the workload can be too much for a person to handle and thus, we make teams. A team is more than just a group of people. It is an organization.

Every member has a role to play to ensure the team is working at its full potential.

Take note the key elements of a team are communication, vision, and trust.

These elements form the team culture and help to act as the glue keeping the team members together.

Behind every successful project, there is a team of highly motivated and engaged people who are responsible for what they do. It isn't because they have to but because they want to.

Having a solid team culture with strong foundations is crucial for you to build a strong team.

The team culture is what defines a team.

It is team culture which new members notice.

Team culture includes the way communication is done, all of the process to reach goals, the overall vision of the team, level of cooperation, and such.

So, how to build team culture?

Building strong teams which are focused on collaboration can lead to success.

A team which is willing to take ownership of their contribution and know how to work together is what will drive a project toward success. Do not underestimate the importance of building a great team culture.

"In studies by the Queens School of Business and by the Gallup Organization, disengaged workers had 37% higher absenteeism, 49% more accidents, and 60% more errors and defects. In organizations with low employee engagement scores, they experienced 18% lower productivity, 16% lower profitability, 37% lower job growth, and 65% lower share price over time. Importantly, businesses with highly engaged employees enjoyed 100% more job applications."
- Emma Seppala and Kim Cameron

As a team leader, you might find yourself working with an already created team. This means you have to adapt your preconceived ideas to fit the preferences and abilities of the said existing team.

Other times, you will be given the opportunity to create a team.

Regardless of the type of situation you find yourself in, below are some ways you can start building a positive team culture.

The Bigger Vision

An essential component of developing a strong team is having a group of individuals who are focused on a collective effort which happens to be greater than themselves. They need to believe in the bigger vision.

You shouldn't be forcing others to be part of a team. That won't work in the long run. People should have the desire to belong to your team and contribute what they can.

As the leader you should clearly articulate a vision and how the team will achieve it. By understanding the bigger vision, your team members will show more participation.

Take note this isn't a one-time thing. Reinforcing the bigger vision has to be continually reinforced. As the leader you need to infuse this purpose throughout the duration of a project.

Regular Meetings

Having regular meetings can make a big difference in creating great team culture. Such meetings aid in building rapport, encouraging productivity, and bringing the importance of improving the team, and how every member is essential, to the forefront.

Of course, you should schedule such meetings in advance. Everyone should also be familiar with the agenda before the meeting begins. You should have clearly defined roles for meetings to foster better team culture because everyone will be on the same page.

Creating Leaders

According to experts, a great team culture is one which emphasizes mentorship over management.

Cultivating leadership does play an important role in establishing the culture of the team.

You should encourage team members to be their own leaders (in some capacity). Allow them to participate in creating schedules and offering constructive feedback.

Lead by example. Be the leader you would want to lead you. Treat others with respect and you will see the team members do the same.

Knowing Your Team

You can't have a great team culture without knowing who is who. Knowing team members will help strengthen your team's communication, trust, and respect toward one another.

A great team culture is one where members are looking forward to celebrating birthdays, promotions, achievements, and such. It is all about fostering camaraderie even if it is as simple as eating lunch together.

A Culture of Learning

You should promote a culture of learning. Every team member should be encouraged to improve their skills for the betterment of the team.

You can do this by providing access to ongoing training and personal development. Online learning has made it easier for everyone to remain up-to-date. So, offer access to online courses and create opportunities for team members to take on new responsibilities.

Encouraging learning helps prevent team members for feeling bored. It also feeds their curiosity.

Having a strong team culture means you have a team which has a sense of ownership in the planning, problem-solving, and goal-setting processes. They know what is required of them and they are more than willing to step up to the plate.

Developing a great team culture will open doors to success and even attract more talent. It is important to always remember at the heart of every great team are people. Treating your team as capable people instead of just resources is what will help you create an impressive team culture by giving rise to a sense of community.

Chapter 11: The Importance of Setting Team Rules

Due to you having to deal with a number of individuals in a team, it is important for you to set certain team rules to avoid issues that may arise.

How a team makes decisions, assigns work, and holds members accountable are what can determine whether or not the team is successful.

That is why building team relationship guidelines is essential. These guidelines can help shape the culture of the team as they continue working on a project.

Start with understanding what is meant by team norms.

Team norms are a set of rules or guidelines a team establishes to help shape the interaction of its members with one other as well as with employees (external to the team).

It is recommended you help develop team norms during the first meeting. More norms can be added in upcoming meetings down the line.

Team norms are to be used to guide the behavior of team members as well as to assess how well team members are interacting.

These guidelines should be in place to help team members call each other out on any behavior which is deemed inappropriate.

Some basic team norms you should know about are:

- All team members are equal.

- Team members will speak respectfully to each other.

- Team members will listen without interrupting during meetings.

- Team members will make certain they have agreement on what and when to communicate.

- Complaints about team members will be addressed first among team members.

Of course, team norms can be expanded depending on the needs of a team and what is best for the project to be a success.

As mentioned, begin with a few and then add from there when necessary.

Chapter 12: Benefits of Team Building Exercises

I have mentioned team building activities before in this book.

Team building exercises are all about improving or growing a team.

They are about understanding, appreciating, and developing a bond with fellow team members.

A strong bond within the team is what makes a team successful.

For those who aren't familiar with them, let's go over some of the benefits of team building exercises.

Team work

Team building activities help create the time to focus on the importance of teamwork. It shows everyone what is required to create a better team.

Learning how to work together effectively creates efficiency and knowledge on how to manage strengths and weaknesses in a team.

Communication

Again, good communication is vital for a high performing team. Such activities can take down barriers in communication. They boost verbal and nonverbal communication within a team.

Leadership

Structured team building activities help identify leadership qualities in individuals. They also let you, the manager, know about individuals who can serve as leaders in certain instances depending on the type of work they do.

Fun

Having fun as a team is important for building great team culture and such activities offer just that. They showcase the value of having fun in the workplace (when appropriate).

Responsibility

Every member of a team has a specific role. Team building activities help reinforce how taking responsibility and providing responsibility are vital contributors to team performance.

Trust

Having trust is essential in a team. Through such exercises, team members are able to learn more about each other in a more comfortable environment. Getting to know about each other's capabilities makes for a stronger team.

You can see for yourself how team building activities can benefit a team by boosting communication, trust, respect, loyalty, support, and more.

So, give certain team building activities a try to create great team culture.

Check out the Team Building Toolkit from University of California, Berkeley, for some fun ideas.

Chapter 13: Evolving Your Team & The Future

You might have noticed this too... the business landscape is rapidly changing across industries due to demographic changes and evolving technologies.

Organizations need future-thinking leaders to manage teams.

What will the leaders and managers of 2020 and beyond look like?

Well, here are some of the key skills and attributes the leaders of tomorrow will need to thrive.

According to experts, towards 2020 the workplace will continue to evolve in accordance with demographic trends, the changing attitudes towards work, and yes, greater cultural diversity.

Workplaces are becoming more diverse (especially across age groups), and in the future, it is possible a leader might find themselves managing as many as five generations in a team.

Furthermore, leaders are likely to see themselves handling people with short tenures.

The traditional hierarchical structures of organizations will also change. It is more about openness and collaboration between different branches of a business.

Current workplaces, as well as those in the future, tend to value employee engagement as much as performance management. The leaders of tomorrow need to be accepting of other viewpoints. Leaders will be more of guides for teams instead of completely authoritative figures.

Successful leaders and managers will be those who step outside of their comfort zone and welcome, as well as drive, change.
As agents of change, leaders of the future will be innovative and creative. They will know how to come up with new solutions to adapt to the changing business landscapes.

They will leverage strategies like cultural fluency and intelligence, innovative team-building, and novel marketing strategies reflecting the new cultural demographics.

The successful leaders and managers of tomorrow are those who can identify and close opportunity gaps in their market and stay ahead of competition.

They will be willing to broaden observations to find opportunities and exploring new frontiers for growth of the business.

Furthermore, they will also have a comprehensive understanding of technology applications, capabilities, and trends.

Traits like accountability, transparency, fairness, and honesty will continue to be important. They will be out-centric leaders who are focused on developing their teams.

Leaders of tomorrow will be those who are open to change.

Chapter 14: Tips for Managing Team Stress

Stress!

It is something you need to address if you want your team to remain productive.

According to research, in today's workforce, more than a third of Americans experience chronic work stress, while only 36% report they are provided the resources to help them manage their stress at work.

Take not the stress team members feel isn't just a personal issue.

How your team feels at work can have a big impact on productivity, engagement, and even your bottom line!

Taking steps to reduce team stress can bring business up. According to data, happy employees are 20% more productive, and employee happiness has been shown to improve sales by 37%.

There are effective ways you can handle team stress.

Tough Love Doesn't Always Work

Yes, everyone has their own management style, and that is okay. However, if you generally take a tough love approach as a leader, you may be doing more harm than good. According to research, putting negative pressure on employees or showing "tough love" has been found to lead to higher levels of work-related stress, resulting in higher rates of employee turnover and poorer performance.

Try and focus on leading with empathy. Try to look an issue from the perspective of the team member and see how you can offer constructive feedback without sounding too bossy.

Mindfulness workshop

Mindful Meditation reduces anxiety and even changes your brain. The more you meditate, the less ACTH (stress hormone) is likely to exist in your blood. You are also likely to add more gray matter to your brain.

See if there is a local community or yoga center that can help you host such a workshop in the workplace to benefit the team.

Even a few minutes of meditation a day can help with managing stress.

Healthy Snacks

Make healthy snacks available to your team. Many people feel stressed when they are hungry. By allowing them to eat healthy snacks you won't just be fulfilling their cravings, but will also be helping their bodies to not feel stressed.

And yes, chocolate makes people happier. It is just science! Why not allow your team to eat a piece of dark chocolate a day to keep stress away?

Eating 1.4 ounces of chocolate a day (which is a little less than one chocolate bar) has been found to reduce stress and anxiety compared to other foods.

Breaks

Taking breaks can help teams feel refreshed and even work faster. Allow your team to step away from their work for a few minutes to recharge.

Organized Workplace

Having an organized workplace can also help reduce stress. Why not make it a DIY project for everyone?

Set some time aside and work as a team to clean up desks. Seeing a tidy workplace can help the brain feel less stressed out and not grow frustrated when certain files and documents can be found on time.

Team Building Activities

As mentioned, participating in team building activities don't just allow the team to grow stronger, it is also fun and thus helps the team distress.

Honest feedback

As a leader, you might not be aware of all the stress being experienced by team members. Different people handle stress in different ways. That is why it's important to know how the team members are feeling. You need to help them before they burn out or hit a breaking point.

You can set aside some time each month to talk to every member one-on-one. You can ask how they're doing and try to see if they are feeling overstressed due to professional or personal reasons. Ask for honest feedback and let them know you are available to help them.

Switch things up

It can be easy to fall in a routine. So, consider switching things up a bit. You can give team members to assign themselves a different role for the day. For example, if they've been working behind the scenes in the backend coding department, perhaps have them take a shot at frontend development? It'll help them have a better understanding and appreciation for their coworkers.

Chapter 15: Team Building Issues

I can't close this book without talking about team building issues you will face. You need to be familiar with such issues so you can be capable of forming the best team possible.

When you bring a group of diverse individuals together to form a team, challenges such as communication and relationship issues are to be expected.

Putting a team in place isn't enough.

The dynamic and complex nature of what it means to be a team needs a strong and decisive leader for guidance.

Lack of Diverse Skills and Interests

You should know that if an entire team consists of members with similar skills and interests, it might not be the best team out there. You should consider the scope of the project before selecting team members. Doing so will help you choose team members who have a range of different skill sets and interests for more innovative thinking and allowing a team to address an array of issues.

Poor Communication

It's your friend 'Good Communication' again!

When individuals work as part of a team, the importance of communication during all phases of the project can't be stressed enough. If a team member happens to treat their role as an independent one, communication suffers. Furthermore, if the team leader doesn't communicate with the team members, the flow of the project suffers.

To avoid such an issue, you should hold regular team meetings (preferably one every week). You should also ask team members to share their successes and challenges to gauge the level of communication.

You can also make use of certain team management tools to ensure everyone is one of the same page.

Lack of Leadership

Teams need leaders to offer a sense of purpose and direction. Lack of effective leadership only goes to challenge effective team development. Without a strong leader, the said team is likely to lose morale and momentum.

You need to offer your support to the team as the leader. If you are unable to be present during team meetings, you should appoint a team leader. Also, remember to introduce such a leader and their role to the team. Doing so will prevent competition for the said role from other team members.

Also, as the leader, you should be open to listening. Remember everything I have talked about related to being a good leader, it all applies here, too.

Role Confusion

Even though a team works together to achieve certain goals, every team member needs to know their specific role within the team. If they don't, it will lead to role confusion.

When team members lack an understanding of their specific roles or choose not to follow through with their expected roles, the said team is unable to develop. Certain tasks may end up being repeated or not being completed at all, leading to waste of time, effort, and resource.

You should explain each role, in detail, to team member to avoid confusion. Also, you should monitor team members to make sure they adhere to their assigned role.

Chapter 16: Thank You!

Thank you for deciding to give my book on Team Building a read.
It really is an art if you know about everything that goes into building a team and then ensuring the team you have created is able to work efficiently.

I have tried to share all of the information with you in the easiest manner possible. I hope you were able to learn something from this book.

If you have any questions about this book, feel free to contact me at: emmad.rash@gmail.com

You can also find certain courses I have created on Udemy. They include project management and related topics.

I also have a book available on Amazon about Project Management.

Again, thank you for picking up this book. I hope it serves you well!

Other Works by Mekhal Aly

Due to this being a Two-In-One book publication, from here, the Project Management Book will begin.

A Kindle version of the Project Management Book is available, too.

Thank you for reading!

Project Management: Make Every Project a Success Story

Chapter 1: Welcome and Introduction

Hello everyone!

My name is Mekhal Aly, and I welcome you to my book on Project Management.

Have you ever wondered about the term project management? Considering you are now reading this, it'll be safe to assume you have.

According to statistical data, more than 90% of the organizations are in need of capable project managers and project management plans to become successful.

> *In a sense, project management is what can break or make a business.*

You need to understand the importance of project management and by relation the significance of a project manager to be able to offer help to certain organizations and make them excel or improve.

That is why I decided to create this book because I wanted to help teach you all what is meant by project management and why it is such a useful skill to learn. It is the kind of skill which you can apply in any type of business space, academic purposes, or even in your personal life because of some hobby or a DIY project you want to complete.

Everything needs proper management for it to be successful. This is why you must have an understanding of the basics of project management which can help you become better in various aspects of your life.

So, what is project management? Let's start from there.

Basically, project management consists of specific steps.

The first one is the analysis and the overall planning, then comes the execution, the monitoring process, and then knowing how to bring the project to fruition or completion in an efficient manner.

Now, of course, you will see a few changes in the context these five steps are being used in because I will be covering project management to help you understand it in terms of businesses like running a web agency, for example, or creating a mobile app or even managing a grocery store, academics (like how you can use project management skills to help with your syllabus and prepare for exams), and even for more personal stuff such as managing monthly home expenditures.

Later in this book, I will be talking about the role of a project manager, analyzing the resources required for getting a project started, how to motivate your team, understanding the importance of caring about yourself and others you are working with, the challenges you are likely to face, and more.

As for what you will get to learn from this Project Management book, I will elaborate in the next chapter.

I have tried to keep everything simple for you all. The things I cover will help you learn about the role of a project manager and what is expected of them. You will also get to know about the different project management styles you can opt for as well as some project management tools you can consider using.

The other skills and values you will learn include team management and addressing concerns your team might have. How to handle specific challenges that might come up. Knowing the proper ways to monitor a project. Being ready for any changes that might need to be made, and more.

Right now, some of you might probably be thinking there seems to be a lot this book will cover and you might not have the skills to handle all of the information let alone implement it.

Well, here is the good news!

You don't need any pre-requisite skills or knowledge for you to begin learning from this project management book. I have got you covered by sharing everything in the simplest manner possible.

If you are looking to get better in your professional life, you should know almost all of the organizations out there are of the opinion project management is vital for success.

Improper project management doesn't only mean a project won't be completed, it also means the waste of time and resources, especially money.

And no one wants that, right?

Also, considering how vital project management is for organizations, you can also work towards a career as a project manager where you manage projects as a freelancer or as a traditional hire. I will be going over both branches in this book.

So, let's start!

Chapter 2: Importance of a Project Manager

So, first things first. Who is a project manager?

As the name implies, it is anyone who manages a project. In a sense, everyone is a project manager, even if the said project is your life. Being more specific, let's talk about what a person does when they wish to achieve something.

They think of a plan or an idea and then come up with a way to execute the said idea for the desired result which also includes whether or not you have the time or money to do what you wish to do.

For example, let's say you plan to go on to vacation in a foreign country. You can't just get up and leave, right?

You will need to have a plan to go about the entire thing. There are tickets to be paid for, getting a visa, having enough money to spend, hotel reservations, making sure you don't have any pending work, especially if certain deadlines are approaching and more.

You will need to handle this systematically. You will need to first plan the process, think about the places you wish to visit, how many days you wish the trip to last, see what tickets are available, schedule the flights, book rooms, and such.

During the project management process, specific changes are made to ensure the continuation towards success which also includes being motivated… and yes, sometimes failure occurs which helps makes you better prepared for your next try.

This is very true for DIY projects. You think of what you want to make, do a bit of research about what you need, work on the project to complete it, and voila be the proud creator of whatever the project was. Along with the success of the project, you gain experience which makes you better equipped to do the same thing, or even something similar, in the near future.

Now coming over the technicalities of it, here's the definition I took from our friend Wikipedia:

"Project managers have the responsibility of the planning, procurement and execution of a project, in any undertaking that has a defined scope, defined start and a defined finish; regardless of industry. Project managers are the first point of contact for any issues or discrepancies arising from within the heads of various departments in an organization before the problem escalates to higher authorities. Project management is the responsibility of a project manager. This individual seldom participates directly in the activities that produce the end result, but rather strives to maintain the progress, mutual interaction and tasks of various parties in such a way that reduces the risk of overall failure, maximizes benefits, and minimizes costs."

This sounds like a lot of work, right? But don't worry. Being equipped with the right tools and skills can help make your project manager job easier.

Projects can be big or small. A project can be about creating an app, launching a website, even organizing a birthday event. If you think about it, there are a lot of examples of similar projects that pop up in our daily lives, and even unknowingly we are acting as project managers.

Knowing how to go about not only getting the project approved, but also keeping in mind the time, money, and workforce required, and then giving rise to an environment which increases the chances of success is all a project manager's job.

You will need to create schedules and even decide if you wish to use specific project management tools.

As I have mentioned, companies credit project management for their success because they understand the real value of project management which I will be going over next.

The Real Value of Project Management

Let's talk about the real value of project management. Also, a quick note for those looking to begin a career as a project manager, during the interview you can be asked the same question... what is the value of the project manager?

We all have an idea about what value means in this context. It means importance or worth. You know, how useful something or someone is.

The value of project management has to do with how it can help deliver consistent results along with increases the efficiency of the entire process. It is related to everything. Good project management practices can help reduce costs, even get the project completed on time, improve team motivation, and lead to many advantages for an organization.

The project manager is one who knows how to deliver these promises through project management. They plan and direct the work for the team. They monitor the progress and are ready to course correct the project if a challenge arises.

Knowing a project is being handled by a capable project manager is why organizations are ready to pay project managers. And I am talking being paid a lot of money here, which I will get to later in this book.

Some of the benefits of a capable project manager are:

- Clear project objectives
- Knowing what to expect
- Efficient execution
- Being able to handle issues that arise
- Keeping the team in check

From my experience as a project manager... I talk to the head of the organization the project is being done for. We discuss the expected results. The costs and funding. The team working on the project. We also go over the deadlines of the milestones, and the expected date of completion. And then I move from there to ensure everything is running smoothly.

As for my experience with launching websites, I talk to the client about what they wish the blog or website to look like. I then come with a budget that will be needed to have a developer begin working on it. The budget also includes funds for the team maintaining the website, handling the content and such.

Furthermore, I also work with the content team to create content which will be posted on the website upon launch. Not only that, but I even come up with a schedule for the social media team so they can begin hyping the upcoming launch of the website. It helps to create milestones and going in a systematic manner. You'll understand what I mean as you continue with this book.

As for what many of you will encounter, especially working for a business, the important thing for a project manager to do is understand the pain points. Once the pain points have been listed, you can propose a project to help eliminate or decrease the pain point. You could also suggest a way to increase profits and such.

As a project manager, you need to tell an organization about the value of your project management skills. This is because they understand the importance and value of project management. However, they need to know what you can bring to the table if you wish to be given charge of the said project.

Different Kinds of Projects

In this part, I will be talking about the different kinds of projects you might end up managing as a project manager.

You might want to work on a physical project or perhaps a virtual one. I have had experience with both kinds and both need some changes in the way you handle things if you wish to be successful.

Now, by physical projects, I mean you might be doing something physical such as redecorating a building, crafting something, and more. As for the virtual projects, that has more to do with the online or virtual world such as launching a website or an app. Different kinds of projects need different kind of resources for completion.

And yes, sometimes both physical and virtual aspects can be part of a single project.

With every project there is going to be a team involved and in that team there are going to be people with different skills and temperaments. As a project manager you will need to know how to work with the team you are given. But more on that later.

As for the projects, they could be of a professional kind where you are hired by an organization to oversee a project. This could be something like designing a logo or even launching a new product or service.

There are also academic projects. These have to deal with academic research and making sure everything is being done under appropriate time. Going towards the non-professional side of things, you might find yourself being a project manager while you are a student.

Then there are personal or DIY projects. This could be working with someone to build a new patio or a shed, or even a treehouse. I just wanted to mention personal projects to link with what I said at the beginning of this course about how everyone has served the role of a project manager in one way or another.

Going forward with this book, I will be focusing more on professional project management; however, the skills and tips I will share can also be utilized in academic and personal projects to increase the likelihood of success.

Chapter 3: Managing a Project from Start to Finish

Before you go about managing a project, you need to know how to begin a project. As a project manager, you are expected to know the best way to not only plan a project but to also get it off the ground.

Let's go to the steps I mentioned during the beginning.

- **The Analysis and Planning**

Everything starts with an idea, and you need one to initiate a project. Turning the idea for the project into something which can actually be worked on requires many essential factors to be kept in mind. The Analysis and Planning stage is first of them.

Depending on what the organization requires, your ultimate first goal is to get the idea approved by the higher authorities. To get the idea approved, or before you start working on some given project by your boss/bosses, you will need to do your share of research. You will need to analyze the pain points or a certain scenario and come with an idea behind a project to deal with the said pain point or points. You will need to understand why is it important and how it can improve the organization.

For example, keeping it simple, the organization wants to become better at dealing with the responses they get from content published on the website. However, there isn't a comment box present. Instead, customers have to email the organization directly.

As a project manager, you can begin planning a way to convert the emails into a healthy discussion on the website or blog itself which can lead to helping other visitors, too. Giving readers of online content the ability to leave comments can bring forth stronger communication and engagement with the organization.

But who will create the comment box? You'll need to come up with a budget for the developer who will handle such a process in the time you want him or her to work in.

So, you take your plan to the organization's head or anyone who is in charge. You tell them about the importance of having a comment box and why a budget is necessary. To be able to have a project approved you have to be able to convey its importance.

Of course, you will also have to talk about spam comments being left behind or even certain bad comments which can harm the company's reputation. So, as a project manager, who is expected to know about risks, you will talk about having a customer support team ready to address such comments in a timely manner and do damage control. Again, you will need to come up with a budget for that, too.

You will also need to come up with a plan related to how the said project will be completed. It doesn't have to be too in-depth. The basics of a plan are enough to help you get a project approved. You need to have clear objectives. You also need to have a budget in mind and the resources required. The more at ease you can make an organization feel, the better the chances of you getting a project approved.

Forming a team is important, too. You need to have team members who have the skills you require for a project to be completed on time.

I can't stress the importance of the planning phase enough. For example, a client wishes for an app to be created. They know what they want the app to do and they want you to make it a reality. Even during the planning phase of such a scenario, you will need to look at the team you will be working with.

Does the client already have a team in mind? Do they expect you to make some calls and gather a team with the skills needed to handle such a project?

Furthermore, you will need to create the schedules for the team to follow. You will need to know which tasks need to be assigned to which member of the team. Prioritizing tasks is vital, too. And you need to have a budget so all of the resources (Hardware and Software) you will require can be made available.

Depending on when the client wants the app, you will have to keep in mind the time duration of not the entire project but also which task needs to be completed by what time.

Once you are done with the analyzing phase, you will take your proposal to the client for approval. Upon approval is when you can begin the execution phase.

Think of the planning phase as the backbone of the entire project. It is the blueprint which is to be followed to ensure a project's success.

If the planning phase isn't up to par, how can you expect the project to run smoothly? From the scheduling to the milestones to even having backup plans if something goes wrong, it's no wonder organizations weigh the value of a project manager by looking at what he or she is capable of doing during the planning phase.

- **The Execution**

Once everything has been planned, you can go on ahead to the execution phase. This is the point where you work on the project. You are responsible for setting up everything which can be required for the project.

For example, an organization requires a new logo. During the planning phase, you should have gone over the resources you would require, like the software to be used for the logo or even the system the designer will use. The execution phase is when the work begins on the project.

If it's physical construction work, you have gone over the tools and materials the team will need and the budget depending on how much they will cost. You then hand everything to the team, and they execute the plan to start working on the project.

The team begins their work according to the schedules you have provided them. They can also use any project management tools you might have recommended. During the execution phase, it is crucial you have laid the foundations of positive communication between you and the team.

- **The Monitoring Process**

As the name implies, this is a very important phase where you monitor the progress of the project. Having certain milestones set up for a project can make the monitoring process more comfortable for you. As a project manager, you will need to monitor everything. Having a system which you can use to track everyone's progress in an efficient manner is vital.

Take the mailing service for example. They give you a tracking number or ID which you can use to see when a parcel has been shipped, when it will be delivered, etc. Similarly, you will need to keep an eye on the team, knowing which tasks they are working on, how much progress they have made, when will they begin on the next task and so on.

Having an efficient monitoring process let you prioritize work as well as know how to handle the situation if a deadline nears and certain things have to changed. You can also think of the monitoring stage as a precautionary system. You can use it to call meetings and see if the team is on the right track, seeing red flags and immediately maneuvering the project's progress as needed.

You will need to keep an eye on how the funds are being used, which team member is at what stage of their work, how the entire team is progressing towards the milestones, whether or not deadlines are being met, and so on.

You will also need to ensure issues are being addressed in an appropriate manner during this process to keep everything streamlined. Again, communication with the team and keeping things transparent, especially from their end, is vital.

- **The Closing**

The final step is, of course, bringing the project to a close. I have seen many projects have a fantastic start. However, down the line, they end up facing many issues due to poor project management practices. They just don't get completed.

As a project manager, you have to make sure everything is in proper order as the completion deadline comes closer. Double-check to see all of the requirements have been met. Maybe you have worked on launching a website. Then you should have an editor go over the content to make sure it is the best it can be.

Have a checklist to help you judge if the main objectives of a project have been met before you declare it to be finished.

Again, working on projects, even if they aren't a 100% successful will leave you with beneficial experience which can help you better tackle the same project or a similar one down the road.

Chapter 4: Skills Required by Every Project Manager

With everything else in this world, a specific role requires certain skills for you to be good at what you are supposed to do. The same holds true for a project manager. As mentioned in this book, a project manager is one who has to think of the proper strategy to get a project started and then be able to keep the team going to achieve certain milestones and finally, completion.

There are going to be challenges, and a project manager needs to have the skills to address these challenges in an efficient manner.

1. **Communication**

The first skill I am going to talk about is communication.

As a project manager, you require communication skills. You will be answerable to the organization you are working for as well as be a guide or a leader for the team working on the project. Things won't be able to go smoothly if you aren't able to communicate correctly.

To have good communication skills you will need to be a good listener. You can't always talk about what you want and how a project should be handled. You need to take the time to listen to the team you will be managing.

Keep in mind to listen from a place of curiosity to understand someone else's perspective. When it comes down to it, what matters is what people hear and not what you meant to say. As a project manager, be concise and clear when communicating.

Being human, conflicts in your team are likely to arise. It might annoy you, but you need to handle the situation professionally. Listen to both sides and be unbiased in your decision making.

Furthermore, have an open line of communication. By this I mean, team members shouldn't hesitate to talk to you because they feel afraid or something similar. Don't make the team feel they can't come to you with any questions or queries they might have regarding a task.

Always remember 'assumptions' aren't always your friend.

Do not 'assume' someone will do a task correctly. Be sure of everything. Make sure the instructions and specifics of a task have been delivered clearly and let the team know you are always there to address any questions they might have.

Now, even if you present yourself like that as a project manager, even then certain team members might not approach you. That is why it is recommended you hold weekly (or even twice a week… perhaps even more), meetings with the team where they can talk about their progress as well as particular issues they might be facing.

Fun fact, Steve Jobs has been known to hold a meeting once a week.

2. Be a Problem Solver

As a project manager, you are expected to be a problem solver. When starting on a project idea, you are supposed to be one who understands how certain pain points can be solved. Similarly, during the execution phase (as well as other phases) of a project, you are expected to solve problems that might arise related to the team you are working with, unexpected delays, and a whole lot more.

As a problem solver, you need to understand the root of the said problem. As a leader, you are supposed to look at something from all angles and then know the best route to take. It is also important to not be too hard on yourself.

There are going to be times you will have to use the 'trial-and-error' route. And doing so is just part of making yourself a better project manager.

Also, don't let the problem-solving process get to you. You can't lose your cool. You're someone the team looks up to, and you have to continue being strong. Keeping your motivational levels high during those time consuming and potentially hair-pulling moments will trickle down to the team, and they will feel motivated, too.

Don't hesitate to ask help from some you trust when it comes to solving certain problems.

3. Be Ready for Anything

Yes, you made an entire step-by-step plan for a project. Good job!

However, not everything is going to do according to plan. Always be ready for the unexpected. From my experience, I have seen project managers who always have a safety net be the ones who succeed.

A portion of funding might be lost. Illness might strike. The list of events is long. So, don't be strict about the entire thing. Give yourself and the team some breathing room or flexibility. Schedules might have to be changed. Accommodations might need to be made. As a project manager, you will need to know how to cope with all of this.

You can also think of this as risk management. Being able to predict issues that might arise and have plans to address them is a skill every project manager should have. Some people don't think about risks 'that may happen' because they seem unlikely. However, being ready for anything can help you increase your chances of being a proud manager of a successful project.

Being pro-active can help you. If a deadline for a task is on Friday, you can tell the team to do the work by Wednesday or at least by Thursday. This will give you an extra day to handle the task if something happens like someone falling ill or the weather being too bad for people to come to work.

4. Don't be Afraid to Make Decisions

As a project manager, you need to have decision-making skills. As the leader, there are going to be times you will need to make tough decisions. There are also going to be times you will make decisions without consulting anyone. So, you need to be ready to handle such issues without putting them up a vote.

Understanding when and how decisions should be made is important. Your experience can help with better decision making. And even if it's your first time, don't worry about it. Do you research or trust your gut, whatever works for you!

Just don't let your ego get in the way. Don't make decisions because you have the power. Doing so isn't going to do you any good in the long run.

Being decisive is also what the team wants. Everyone likes a leader who knows what they want and is sure about what they do. This inspires confidence in everyone working on a project.

And yes, I am a big advocate of asking for help. Don't hesitate to ask for help from your colleagues or a mentor. It all depends on the scenario you are dealing with.

5. **Personal organization**

For you to get the results you want, you also need to make sure you, on a personal level, are up to standard. Think of it this way... how can you expect to create schedules for others and keep everything organized when you don't have a hold on things at your end?

Being organized in your personal life helps have a positive impact on those working under you. Now, of course, there are going to be certain relationship troubles that can pop up. However, an efficient project manager knows how to organize everything... keeping their personal life and professional life separate, and thus, not allowing any stress from their personal life to trickle into their professional zone and negatively affecting the project's management.

Wrapping up this portion, being a project management means you will need to bring a number of skills to the table. With experience, you will be able to hone these skills and become better at your craft.

Chapter 5: Let's Work on a Project!

Knowing the Pre-requisites – Planning a Project

So, let's get ready to work on a project as a project manager.

Beginning with the first step I have mentioned in this book, you need to start with the analysis and planning phase.

Remember I talked about the pain points? Knowing about the pain points and the coming up with an idea to address them fall under the planning phase.

As a project manager, you will need to make sure you are looking at everything. What I mean by this is sometimes people only focus on the idea and don't necessarily spend time thinking of the budget, time, and other resources required to make a project successful or approved.

What makes a failed project?

It is one that is unable to deliver what is required from it related to the main objectives, being in the set budget, overall quality, and more.

Again, I can't stress the importance of the planning phase enough. Whether you're creating an app or installing a new department space for an organization, you need to handle all of the related teams in an efficient manner. You need to know your budgeting. Talk to the teams and take their feedback when it comes to how much time they need to deliver what's expected of them. Set the schedules. Only with a well thought-out planning phase can you expect the project to become a success.

You will need to broaden your approach if you wish to be a good project manager. Take time to analyze the situation. Do your research and then come up with an idea or plan. Then work on writing out how the said plan can be executed. Again, this includes the resources you require, the team you will need to work on, and how much time is required.

Working on being ready for certain risks that might occur is also part of an efficient planning phase. Don't think that just because the project is too small, you won't face any risks. Don't be like that. Have a contingency plan for unexpected budgetary limitations, falling behind on certain deadlines, team members being reassigned, or certain changes which have to be made.

Also, there might be instances where you will be working with a project planning team. An organization might give you a pre-decided planning team, or you might be asked to create a planning team yourself. When you are working with a planning team, it is important for you to keep an eye out with regards to what's working and what isn't.

Whether you are building something, changing something which already exists in an organization, or launching a new blog or a promotional campaign, the planning phase is very important. If you plan things out correctly, the chances of encountering delays during the execution and monitoring phases lessen.

Let me share some tips which can help you make the project planning process better.

Tips for an Efficient Project Planning Process

1. **Analyzing the Planning Process**

Just because you are a project manager doesn't mean you can't evaluate the planning process you come up with. Always be ready to ask yourself questions about 'why' you want to go about a project the way you want to.

During the planning process ask yourself what is and what isn't working. There is no shame in realizing you might have made a certain mistake during the planning process.

It is better to address such issues and change them at this stage instead of ignoring it or assuming everything will be okay and then facing a major issue down the line. Don't rush it.

Ask people you trust for feedback. The better your plan, the easier executing the project should be.

Some of the things you can do include:

- Developing a business plan template
- Evaluating the strengths and weaknesses
- Establishing measurable objectives for each goal
- Designating the participants in the process

If you are working with a planning team, again, communication is very important. Also, make sure the team members have experience for the project being planned. Observe them. Know if they are focusing too much on the creative side of things or if they are being too analytical about the process. You will have to be the one to bring balance to the team.

Also, look at how many steps are involved in the completion of a process. Are there certain steps you can take out? Can the project continue if a certain step doesn't work?

Furthermore, look at the tools being used. Is the project team experienced with handling such tools or is time needed to train them properly?

I will be talking about the use of project management tools as you continue with this book.

2. Reach Out

By this, I mean reaching out to the team that will be working on the project. As a project manager, there will be times you can easily be in contact with a single member of a team who will go on to convey your instructions to others.

A good way to boost team morale and making everyone feel like an important part of a project is by reaching out to them yourself.

During the planning process, identify the roles of team members yourself. Let them know about the tasks they will be handling and why they are important for the said project. Handout schedules yourself and be open to any comments the team members might have.

Simplify the process for them. Set the rules. Make them see the vision you have so everyone is on the same page.

Being a project manager who doesn't seem to be interested in connecting with team members might not be a good idea if you wish to be successful at your job.

3. Planning Team Meetings

Chalk out how you will be planning team meetings during the initial planning process instead of trying to work out the specifics once the project has started. During the monitoring process, it is important you stay updated with regards to the progress being made.

So, how to plan team meetings?

- Make sure about who is being asked to attend a meeting. There are instances where the wrong people are asked to attend the wrong meeting. This leads to wastage of their time and them leaving the meeting wondering what they were even doing there.

- You also need to make sure the required people are notified about a team meeting beforehand. Ask yourself if you will be sending out text messages or emails to notify the team.

- Also, share the purpose of the meeting, so attendees know why they are being asked to be there. This allows them to understand if there is certain information or data they are expected to provide during a meeting. Having members be prepared for a meeting can lead to better productivity and participation during such discussions.

- You also need a game plan for a meeting. Knowing beforehand what you will be covering in a meeting helps to save everyone's time.

- Be clear about how many times a team meeting will be held. It could be once a week or even twice a month. Of course, this might change depending on the requirements of a project, but having an idea about how many meetings will be held, how long they will be, and the location they will be held in can help you create a better overall plan for a project.

Give these tips a try and see how they work out for you as a project manager.

Chapter 6: Working with a Team

For your project to be successful, you need to have a team you can rely on. The team you are managing should have all the skills and experience required by the said project. As a project manager, it can fall upon you to select or structure the type of team you want.

The reason I'm elaborating the point about what you need to structure a good team is because an efficient team can lead to a very creative and motivated environment. Brainstorming sessions can give rise to a number of opinions and ideas you might not have thought about. Furthermore, a good team also means less chances of there being conflicts with you as well as amongst the team members.

An efficient team can't be created unless everyone works together. And of course, working together gives rise to a stronger professional relationship and boost overall productivity. Everyone will be ready to support each other. It will be your job as a project manager to make everyone work together, even people who might be smarter than you.

Take note that as a project manager you could end up working with more than one team. For example, you are to act as a project manager for an app an organization wishes to launch. A certain team might be in charge of handling the designing process, another will be working on writing the code, another will be dealing with debugging and testing, while another will be in charge of promotion, and so on.

Knowing that each team is built of people you can rely on will make your job much easier as a product manager.

When you are structuring a team, here are a few things you should consider:

1. **Understand the number of teams you want**

You should plan out the number of teams required to handle the said project. Also, think about the number of members each team will need. As I've mentioned, a project could end up having more than one team. So, ask yourself how you will be able to structure teams, so both the project work and the operational work is handled.

Depending on the nature of the project, you can't simply stop your duties as a project manager at the planning phase. Once the project work has been completed (for example, the app has been created), you will probably have to stick around for the operational work to see the app doesn't have bugs, and then also monitor the promotional progress or anything else required from you.

Similarly, a team might be required to work on hardware while another might be required to work on software. So, make sure you have the teams capable of handling what is needed to make the project a success.

2. **The Geography**

Many organizations hire freelancers to handle a project. So, you might find yourself working with a team that lives all the way on the other side of the globe. That is why when structuring a team, ensure that you are in contact with international teams and everyone is on the same page about what is required for a project, the scheduling, the deadlines, when group meetings are supposed to be held, and so on.

3. **Your Chain of Command**

You also need to look over the chain of command when it comes to structuring a team. By this I mean you need to see if you will be in direct contact with the team members or will you need to go through a CEO, a Director, and such.

For some teams, you might be connected to a person leading the team and for some, you might have to go through the CEO or be in contact with the Director who will then connect you with the team members or a representative.

You should be ready about making such connections. So, go over the chain of command while structuring a team to ensure information is being shared in an efficient manner.

4. **Don't Hesitate to Make Tough Choices**

As the project manager, you are responsible for seeing the project all the way to the finishing line. You need to have a team that can keep up with your demands. That is why it is important to make tough choices while structuring a team.

Go over the resumes of the people that have a chance of being on the team. You need to keep the selection process very professional. Even if you are friends with someone, giving special treatment to them and not selecting someone who is more experienced might not end well for the project as a whole down the line. The better you are at making teams, the lesser the chances of you facing team-related troubles during the progress of the project.

Chapter 7: Building Effective Team Communication

Communication is a key skill for every project manager to have. After you have made teams for the project, you will need to have efficient communication between you and the team to help make the project a success.

Ask yourself, how can you expect to monitor a project when no one really knows what is going on and what is expected of them?

Without proper team communication, different teams might end up doing the same task and waste time and resources. They might not be clear about deadlines or when to join for team meetings, and the list continues.

As a project manager, you are the one who has to give rise to an environment that promotes effective team management.

The office culture has changed over the years. There is a different way to treat teams. There are different expectations and policies that need to be followed. Due to the success of any project being heavily dependent on the team you have, strong communication is vital. Such communication strategies include keeping everyone in the know via technology as well as in person. Depending on the situation, everyone should know what a fellow team member or even a different team working on the same project is up to. And you, as a project manager should be on top it all.

Poor communication can lead to a ton of challenges which add to the other issues you will be facing while working on a project.

Better safe than sorry, right?

You should focus on having a communication channel that works for everyone and also helps build trust and support along the way.

Some of the ways you can give rise to efficient team communication are:

1. **Interact**

I'm talking having in-person, one-on-one interactions. Depending on the nature of the project and number of teams working for it, you can interact with each member in-person and talk to them about your expectations and the tasks they will be handling.

If there are too many people to go through, you can always have a group meeting, before the start of a project, and go over what is required. Being open to such in-person interactions can help foster an environment in which team members feel comfortable working with you because they also know you are willing to listen to them and be fair.

Building on this point, two-way communication is essential. Remember how I talked about being a good listener? You need to continue being one throughout the project's timeline. You should encourage feedback from the team. Let them feel comfortable with bringing their opinions to the table along with any concerns they might have as well.

Allowing feedback from team members also helps make the team self-evaluate. Due to them feeling valued, they are more motivated to focus on the tasks given to them.

You can opt for a one-on-one meeting to interact more with an individual or you can opt for a group meeting to see certain people who aren't participating as much as you would like. You should know how to handle different personalities.

There are different ways you can give rise to such communication and feedback. You can ask them to send you emails when needed. You can also answer calls at specific times. Furthermore, feedback can also be collected during team meetings. You can also use a project management tool to leave feedback on the progress of team members or have the team share their own feedback with you. See which way works for you the best to improve overall communication and productivity.

2. **Appreciation**

There is a saying, treat others how you would like to be treated yourself. Being a project manager gives you a lot of power. However, you shouldn't let the power get to your head. It is unfortunate to see certain project managers not treating teams with respect, thinking they are far better or by giving off an air which shows how they don't have time to deal with the team by responding to their feedback or related issues.

Showing appreciation can go a long way. While improving communication is important, you also need to work on showing appreciation to build an overall positive environment of effective team communication. Making team members feel appreciated for the work they have done and are continuing to do is a good way to keep the morale high.

Small acts can go a long way. Congratulate team members on a job well done. Even a simple thank you can send a very positive message for everyone and keep them motivated.

3. Team building activities

Activities are another fun and effective way to build team communication. Team building activities can help increase productivity and trust between everyone. Good professional relationships can be considered as the backbone for everyone to communicate in the proper manner. As a project manager you should work on conducting activities that help team members to collaborate with each other.

You can have these group activities be conducted during group meetings. Icebreakers are an awesome way for everyone to get to know each other, especially when you are working with more than one team as this helps members from different team get to know each other a bit.

Even a monthly lunch involving everyone can help with building better professional relationships. You need a happy and co-operative team to make a project a success.

4. Allow Teams to Collaborate

If you think it is necessary, you should allow certain teams to collaborate in a more direct manner. For example, let's talk about an app being created. The design team can collaborate with the promotional team and go over what the target audience currently needs and how both teams can work together to deliver something good.

It is all about having a creative atmosphere. Yes, there will be arguments which you will need to bear. You will also need to step in and oppose certain opinions, however, the important thing is to let the team collaborate and evolve.

Also, encourage members of a team to work together to handle certain tasks. The team should be allowed to ask questions and even ask for help from other teams, depending on the context of the situation.

Through a team that understands one another, success can be achieved.

5. The Way You Communicate

You require an effective communication stream for the project to run smoothly. It all comes down to what your project needs. So, plan about how you will be communicating with others. Will you be using emails, making calls, or asking a particular person in each team to convey your message? Perhaps you will be using a project management tool?

See what works for you the best.

Personally, a project management tool can help make communication streamlined. It is also a good way to do away with long email chains and remembering to send particular emails to everyone the information is meant for.

Project management tools can also help you keep up with the progress of the team, and thus aid with the monitoring process, in real-time.

Planning Projects with Your Team

Planning projects with your team can be beneficial for you as a project manager. It allows for more collaboration and insight from others. Of course, there are project managers who want to do all of the planning on their own. However, doing so might not always work for you.

Ask yourself, is planning a project on your own and then presenting it to your team and getting to know about all the things that don't work and waste time better than asking for certain opinions and feedback from the team during initial phase of planning?

Having the team involved in the planning process can help you get better estimates, especially when it comes to knowing how much time a team will need to complete specific tasks.

Getting the team involved also promotes overall communication and makes them feel more invested in what they are working on. The information you will give them will come across as something they will be interested in instead of just being looked at as a set of instructions you wish them to follow.

Let's go over an example. Let's say you are a project manager for an app that's being built. You can ask the design, the coding, and even the testing and marketing teams to come interact with you so you all are on the same page related to how everyone should handle the specific project.

Having such type of collaboration will allow you to take into consideration how much time the coding team requires, how much time the design team needs, and so on to complete the tasks they are handling. Their feedback will enable you to come up with a schedule that works for everyone. And if there are certain changes that need to be made in the schedule due to time constraints, you can work with the teams to figure out the best course of action to ensure the deadlines are met.

Furthermore, being in contact with each team and listening to what they need also leads to a more efficient way to distribute resources as well as how to use the budget allotted or the said project.

Chapter 8: Executing the Project

Once the planning phase is done, you need to head on to the execution phase of a project. There are organizations out there that have experienced their share of issues related to their failure of being able to close the gaps between the strategy they came up with and proper execution.

Even you might face such an ordeal. You might feel very good about the plan you came up with. However, when it is time to execute the plan, things turn out different. Once everyone started working on their individual tasks you get to see things aren't being correctly. The objectives aren't being met and more.

The good news is there are ways you can address such issues and ensure the project execution progresses with not a lot of issues.

In simple terms, project execution is about completing the work that has been outlined in the plan and implementing certain skills and techniques to meet goals. As a project manager, during the execution process, you will have to keep an eye on:

1. Managing the team
2. Following process
3. Communication

As for the execution gap, this can be defined as the gap between the objectives or goals which need to be met and the ability of a team to attain these goals. As a project manager, you need to make sure everyone is on board with what is required so you can decrease the execution gap as much as possible.

Some of the execution gaps you need to be alert for are:

1. Poor Communication
2. Poor Leadership
3. Poor Adaption to Change

Let's begin with the first point... Poor Communication. Your team won't be able to execute a plan in an efficient manner if they don't understand what is required of them. That is why you need to make sure the communication channels between you and the team are open and clear. Proper documentation is very crucial.

As a project manager, your leadership skills are going to have an impact on how a project is executed. Not being able to keep the team motivated or addressing their concerns can lead to poor execution.

And then there is the poor adaptation to change. Issues are going to arise when a project is being worked on. As a project manager, you should be ready to counter any unexpected issues that might arise. You will need to have a Plan B, C, and more to solve certain problems and ensure the execution process continues toward the goals which have been set.

Some tips to improve the Project Execution phase are:

1. **Don't Lose Sight of the End**

You need to have a clear understanding of the project's results or what is expected. Not having clearly defined goals lead to problems during the execution phase. So, make sure you cover all your bases during the planning process of project management. Knowing what needs to be done will help everyone understand how specific tasks should be done.

There will be times a new task or a new change will pop up. You will need to stop yourself from being distracted from your main goal and keep your team occupied in a manner to complete the project. If a new task or change will lead to halting a project's progress, don't hesitate to take it up with the organization and work on how to execute everything properly.

2. **Understanding Across the Board**

Your team needs to have a clear understanding of the project. You should let them know what and how something is supposed to be done. More importantly, you need to let them know why something needs to be done.

Again, efficient communication is vital. Don't hesitate to explain your vision for the project. Giving everyone a deeper understanding about what is being worked on can contribute to better project execution.

Think of it from the team's perspective. How would you feel about working on a project you aren't clear about? You are just given instructions and are expected to meet certain milestones. You won't feel too good about it, right?

Ask your team and give them a chance so they can share whatever they feel about the project and the understanding they have about it confidently.

Letting everyone understand the project at a deeper level allows them to feel more invested in the work they are being asked to do. So, do communicate the necessary information and as a project manager, let the team know you are always here to address any queries they might have.

3. You Are the Leader

You are the project manager! You are the leader that has to get a project across the finish line. You will have to come up with strategies that utilize the team you are working in the most efficient manner possible.

As a project manager you require business management skills along with emotional intelligence and self-awareness. Without having an understanding about yourself, you can't expect to lead others to success. Don't let your ego get in the way of properly executing a project. If you require some help, don't hesitate to ask for it from someone you trust. Perhaps your colleague or a mentor? It is better to get the help you need in time instead of allowing your own lack of a certain skill to increase the execution gap.

Also, you need to be a good listener if you wish to be a good leader and want to close gaps. Don't hesitate to rely on useful feedback from the team you are working with. As a leader there will be times you will need to defend your team in from of the CEO or any other authority you are answerable to. You will need to step up during these times to foster trust and communication.

4. Adapting to Necessary Changes

Many project managers aren't able to close gaps because they are unable to adapt to unexpected issues that might arise during project execution. As a project manager, you will need to be flexible with how you run things. Every project is unique and each comes with its own share of possible risks.

You might not realize certain issues during the planning phase. However, once the execution begins, there can be a number of problems that might arise. And you need to be ready!

The possibility of change can be extremely stressful and scary. But change is the only constant, whether professional or personal, which can be tackled with the right mindset.

As a project manager you should be able to handle such problems and make changes accordingly to ensure the project continues on the path to success. You should be able to pivot the current direction and have the team on board to accept the tactical changes you need to make. Again, proper communication is very important so everyone working on a project know what changes are supposed to be made without wasting too much time or resources.

5. Milestones help

Depending on the size of a project, the entire execution phase might seem like a daunting prospect. One way for you to do away with such a feeling is by dividing it up in small phases.

Take it one milestone at a time.

Seeing the project moving forward and reaching certain milestones will also help everyone involved feel motivated about the job they have done. Furthermore, having milestones will also provide you with a better understanding about what isn't being done... meaning the gap that's present, and you can go ahead and make certain changes to close it.

Monitoring milestones is vital so you can keep everyone in the loop and see overall progress.

Chapter 9: The Challenges You Will Face as a Project Manager

I think this is a good time to address some challenges you will face as a project manager. Managing projects isn't easy. As I've mentioned, you will need to take care of everything.

There's the planning phase, the execution phase, monitoring, ensuring efficient communication, being ready for risks, and the list goes on.

Being human, there is always a chance of something slipping through the cracks while you are trying to do your best as a project manager.

I'm going share with you some of the common challenges you are likely to face as a project manager so you can have an understanding about what you need to be ready for.

1. **Poorly Defined Goals**

One of the challenges project managers and the team they are working with is not being clear about the expectations. That is why the planning phase is vital. It is there where you need to do everything you can to make sure the goals and the objectives are defined.

Everyone needs to know about the 'what, why, and the when' of the project as well as the 'how,' which leads to the execution phase.

As a project manager, don't think you will be able to handle everything even though there is some level of uncertainty when it comes to making expectations clear. Not knowing where a project is supposed to head as well as the final result that needs to be achieved can lead to you wasting money, time, and effort.

So, what is the solution? That is reasonable to ask.

Be realistic!

> "A goal without a plan is just a wish!"

Simply having a goal in mind does not achieve success.

Always take as much time as needed during the project planning phase and have efficient communication to make sure everyone is on the same page. Also, you should consider using a planning software of some kind so everyone has a record of the goals that need to achieved.

Creating a demo or sample is a good way to see if the final goals are realistic. An idea might include reaching quite high. However, when you have a prototype you can see what's realistic and what's not.

It is better to change certain goals during the planning phase instead of trying to achieve unattainable goals just because they seem impressive.

2. Deadlines that Make Sense

One of the ways to measure whether or not a project is failing is by seeing if deadlines are being met. However, a project is bound to fail if you and your team are working with unrealistic deadlines. Such deadlines make everyone struggle because there is a lot being expected of them. Being competitive and wanting to have a project completed earlier is a reasonable decision, however, again, you have to be realistic about the entire process.

So, should you plan deadlines?

Bring the team your working with into the loop. When planning their schedules, you should communicate with them about what they are able to deliver and how much time is required. Is there something you can do to ease the process and make it faster? Is it okay to extend the initial deadline by a few more days and still be able to have the entire project complete on the date the organization expects it to be?

Always have some 'safe days' or a bit more time with you. There will likely be delays, technical issues, members falling ill, and more.

Make use of your time-management skills and see how you can schedule everything so the deadlines are realistic for the team working on a project. Also, go over the progress of your team in real-time to have a better idea about productivity and if everything is on the right track to complete a project.

Furthermore, make use of a planning calendar to keep track of everything. Using such calendars also lets everyone know if deadlines have been changed.

3. Geographically Dispersed Teams

As a project manager, you are likely to work with teams operating from a geographical area different than yours, whether it is a different state or even a different country or continent. Working with such teams mean you have to handle different time zones and even language barriers.

Make sure you are in contact with them during the planning phase and build a confident professional relationship with such teams. Let them know you welcome communication and are here to help them take care of issues as a project manager.

Making such teams clear about what is required beforehand and the way you will be working with them can help decrease a number of challenges which might appear down the line.

Furthermore, create a schedule for meetings, taking into consideration the time zones, in a manner that works for both of you. Also, using a project management tool can help you make things easier for everyone.

4. The Scope Changes

As a project manager, another challenge is how the scope of a project can change when you begin working on it. Everything might seem to be going according the way you want during the initial stages of the planning phase. However, you might notice the project is changing... it seems a lot different than what you imagined as the execution process continues. Such an occurrence is when the scope of a project ends up falling outside the initial objectives you so carefully listed.

Project managers need to understand little changes can end up becoming a big problem down the line. You might consider ignoring an issue, hoping you will be able to fix it later, but then another little issue pops up, and then another one, and then another one, leaving you to deal with more than you can efficiently handle.

A way to counter change in scope is by having very good management skills. If you sense things are changing or are about to change, you should be able to make adjustments to your initial plans in a manner than don't make the project fall way behind the final deadline.

Also, ensure the related team knows about the changes which need to be made. You can set alerts for everyone to keep them informed about what's happening.

As change in scope happens a lot during projects, and there isn't a single solution that is bound to work a 100% for everyone. Making sure you are able to document everything and communicating in an efficient manner can help you keep things under control.

5. Handling Team Issues

The teams or team you serve as a project manager can have issues within the team that lead to the project's progress being hindered. Team members have different personalities and trying to cater to everyone can be a tough thing to handle. Disagreements within the team have to be handled in a professional manner as not to disrupt the work environment.

As a project manager, you will need to ensure a positive work environment for the team. As mentioned, you need to be a good listener if you wish to be a good leader. If a disagreement arises, whether it is inside a team or in between two teams or more, you will have to listen to every side of the story and then present an unbiased solution to everyone involved.

Another good way to ensure disagreements don't end up hindering the project's progress is by involving everyone in team-building activities. Allow team members to mingle in a professional manner during a team coffee break or even a team lunch.

You should promote collaboration between different teams so they can feel comfortable working with each other and better communicate with one another as well.

So, wrapping up this portion, project management is something that requires a lot of skills. Not only that, it also requires you to be patient. You need to be constantly analyzing everything to ensure no hiccups occur. And even if certain issues do arise, you need to be ready to come up with solutions to address them in a proper manner so the project can continue on its path to successfully being completed.

You will need to be pro-active as a project manager. You will need to think of scenarios which might occur during any of the phases of project completion and know the proper ways to counter all of them.

That is why Risk Management is important for a project manager. This means you need to identify, assesses, and then prioritize the risks which might occur and then know what resources or techniques need to be applied to prevent the said risk or to minimize the damage that can occur. It is all about making sure you keep things under control.

One of the things that help differentiate a novice project manager from an experienced one is the ability of an experienced or seasoned professional having skills related to risk management.

Risks can be anything, depending on the kind of project you are working on. The risk might come from the changing financial market. It might be something related to the budget being cut, someone in the team falling ill, transportation issues, weather issues, and more.

It all about being able to think about the unknown and being ready for whatever might come. You need to have a strategic plan for everything that might occur and ways to handle it.

The important thing is not to be too paranoid about it, though. If you, as a project manager, become paranoid, your psychological wellbeing will end up impacting the rest of the people you are working with.

So, taking care of your mental health is important, too. Don't make yourself a risk for the project!

Chapter 10: Tips for Managing Stress as a Project Manager

As a project manager, it is only natural for you to experience some level of stress. You should know stress isn't always bad.

Some might even say if you aren't feeling a bit stressed out as a project manager, you are doing something wrong.

Stress, in small doses, can enable you to perform under all the pressure around you as well as motivate you to try and do your best. However, this is what you need to keep in mind... not being able to manage the stress you are going through and constantly being overwhelmed is going to have a negative impact on your mind and body. And as a project manager, when your body and mind is affected, it is going affect the team you're working with, too.

That is why it is vital you know how to manage stress and bring a balance to your nervous system. The first thing you need to do is recognize the signs and symptoms of stress and then work your way toward proper management.

So, what is stress?

In the simplest of terms, stress is how your body responds to a threat or a demand. When danger is sensed (it can be real or imagined) the defense systems of your body are activated, which is also known as the 'fight-or-flight' response or the 'stress response.'

Such a response is to help your body survive. That's why you feel more alert. The stress response can save your life during emergencies, giving you an adrenaline rush so you can defend yourself and make split-second decisions. It helps your survival instincts to kick in.

For example, making your body jump away from an oncoming vehicle.

However, there is a point where stress stop being helpful to you. It ends up turning into a biological response which needs to be managed to prevent damage to the quality of your professional and personal life.

For those of you who might not know this, our bodies aren't capable of distinguishing between emotional and physical threats.

What I mean by this you can feel stressed due to an argument in the same manner as if you are facing a life-and-death situation. Also, while a life-and-death situation can pass, if you are feeling stressed by something someone said, such kind of stress can go on for days or weeks. Also, the more your stress response is activated, the harder it becomes for your body to shut it down. Again, what I mean by this is if you are stressing out frequently, your body will continue being in a stressed out or heightened stage for most of the time.

Such stress, or chronic stress, can suppress the overall immune system, making you more vulnerable to diseases. It can also lead to problems in your digestive system as well as increase the risk of having a heart attack or a stroke. And yes, even the aging process is rushed. Being under stress can also open doors to cognitive issues related to anxiety, depression, and more.

It's not great to feel stressed when you are a project manager because of the cognitive issues you can face such as:

1. Memory problems
2. Not being able to concentrate
3. Poor judgment
4. Being pessimistic
5. Getting easily irritated
6. Getting easily angry

'Workplace stress' is a real thing and you should know how to manage it properly to become an effective project manager. You could feel stressed out during any or all of the stages involved in project management. Scheduling conflicts might make you feel stressed. Trying to figure out the budget can as well, and so on.

Some tips that can help you manage stress are:

1. **Exercise**

Try and add some kind of workout in your routine. It doesn't have to be much. Regular exercise can help lift your mood and do away with the stress your body has been feeling. Focusing on a workout allows you to keep your worries at bay. Like I said, you don't have to make exercise a burden for yourself. Even going out for a walk can help.

Also, I'm going to talk about it in this section, if you aren't able to exercise, you can go ahead and meditate.

A 10 to 15-minutes long meditation session and help you relax both your mind and body.

It is recommended you exercise or meditate in the morning before heading into work so the relaxed state you're in can help you manage work responsibilities in an effective manner.

2. **Engaging Your Senses**

Another way for you to manage stress is by engaging your senses in a positive manner. You will need to figure out what works for you though. Read some news. Perhaps a tasty cup of coffee? Maybe even reading a book you enjoy? It can even be talking to your friends.

Find what works best for you and take out the time to engage in such activities to help you relax.

3. **Keep an Eye on Your Diet**

I understand how tough being a project manager can be. You might feel so busy because of the workload that you forget to eat properly. The food you eat is linked to your mood. Your diet can worsen or improve your mood. If you're already feeling stressed, eating a lot of processed food such as packets of chips or processed beverages and sugary snacks can heighten stress levels.

So, keeping an eye on your diet can help you manage your body at a physical and cognitive level. Opt for a diet that is rich in fruits and vegetables. Try not to skip meals while you are working on a project. Also, if you wish to snack, go for some baby carrots or something similarly natural instead of picking up the packet of crisps or a few doughnuts near you. A protein bar can help, too.

4. Don't Ignore Rest

Your body and mind needs rest. Looking at what Jeff Bezos, the CEO of Amazon does, he tends to take all of his high-pressure meetings early in morning because that's when his mind and body are fresh. He then moves on to comparatively lighter meetings as the day passes.

Not getting the proper amount of required rest will make you feel cranky and annoyed. When your body feels tired, you experience stress and are unable to think rationally. Also, if you have been feeling stressed out for a while, your sleeping patterns are going to be impacted.

There are a couple of things you can do. As I've already mentioned, you can exercise or meditate to help relieve some of the stress you have been feeling. You can also give yourself a break from all of the work. This is especially important when it is time for you to sleep.

Do not be in bed checking emails on your laptop or cell phone. Keep the gadgets away and focus on falling asleep. A nice warm bath before calling it a day can also help you relax and fall asleep at night. On weekends you can consider going for a long drive or spend some quality time with your loved ones.

While as a project manager you will encounter certain levels of stress, you also need to make sure the team you're working with is also able to manage stress so the project can continue on its path toward success.

Some of the things you can do to help teams manage stress include:

1. **Offering a positive workplace environment** – Making sure there are no distracting noises. The workstations are comfortable, and more. You can talk with the organization if you have any recommendations.
2. **Reasonable demands** – Communicate with the teams so you can work out a schedule that allows the project to be done on time while allowing others to not feel overstressed.

3. **Mutual respect** – Showing respect to the people you are managing also helps to alleviate stress from the overall workplace environment.

4. **Engage** – See if you can schedule group lunches or tea breaks to help everyone relax. Mingle with the team yourself, too. They say laughter is the best medicine. Try and lead by example. You can share a joke or two as icebreakers. Encourage communication and strong professional bonds in the workplace.

5. **Wellness programs** – See if the organization offers workplace health and wellness programs. If they don't, perhaps you can urge them to start?

6. **Breaks** – While making schedules for the teams, make sure you add breaks. Also, if you don't add them, ensure the team leader communicates to the rest of the team the importance of breaks. If possible, set up a room or place where people can go and rest. The said room can even have a bed if needed, and a few games if people are interested in playing them while they unwind.

The project manager and the project team are going to experience stress one way or another. The vital thing is to recognize the signs of stress and then knowing to properly manage stress as not to let it develop further and negatively impact the project's progress.

Efficient communication, and planning everything in advance can help with managing stress. Furthermore, understanding the importance of rest and a proper diet will help, too.

Chapter 11: The Importance of the Monitoring Progress Stage

After the planning phase is done, and the execution of the project has begun for the said project to continue, there comes the monitoring progress stage. You will need to monitor the project to get an idea about how well it is doing.

Monitoring also enables you to decide if certain changes need to be made to avoid possible issues or to accommodate certain changes. You will need to keep an eye on everything to ensure everything is being done on time, the budget isn't being messed up, which milestones and been met and if the upcoming ones can be met in time.

To monitor a project, you will require KPI (key performance indicators) reports from the team or teams working on the project.

- Analyze how many working hours are being put in by teams and if they are what's required to reach certain milestones.

- Ask for budgetary or financial reports. Analyze how much of the funding has been used up and whether or not a certain has had to overspend or is likely to overspend to meet their targets. Always connect the budget with the overall project. What I mean by this is you might be in trouble if almost all of the budget has been used up and you still have more than half of the project to go. So, make sure both, the budget and the project's progress are moving in a manner that will ensure success. Keep a check on the budget for each task or each milestone.

- A good way to go about the monitoring process is by using a project management tool which lets you monitor progress of teams in real-time.

- Team meetings are essential, too. It helps you ask questions about the progress being made. Depending on your schedule, you can have regular one-on-one team meetings, or you can opt for weekly meetings. Having such meetings also helps you understand where each team stands and deal with any issues they might be facing which prevent them from moving forward.

The monitoring stage also involves you having the ability to prioritize. You need to know which tasks need to be fast-tracked so the project can be completed on time.

If an issue does arise during this stage... and it is likely to; you need to be ready to deal with it efficiently. Identify the problem and evaluate the impact it can have.

Should you deal with it right now or can it wait? Is it even something that needs to be dealt with?

If you do decide to handle the issue, do remember to monitor whether or not the solution you implemented was enough to handle the situation.

Again, monitoring and keeping everything on the right track is important.

For example, the project is about creating a new app, and one of the coders falls ill or decides to leave. As a project manager, you will need to come up with a plan to continue the project on track. Going by this scenario, there are a few options available for you.

You can talk to the coding team and see if the unattended work can be divided in a manner that is acceptable and can still help with reaching the deadlines.

Will you need to hire a new employee? Do you have enough time to hire one?

You can also go over the budget of the project and decide to bring onboard a freelancer to take up the space in the coding team that has been created due to a person leaving or being unable to complete their task.

Can you understand why being vigilant during the project's monitoring phase is vital? As a project manager, you will need to have the skills and techniques to go over all of the data you collect during the monitoring process and analyze any issues that might be being faced, or that might pop up later.

You will need to be ready to address issues in time to ensure success. And as I've mentioned many times throughout this book, you need to promote healthy communication, so you know what each team has done, is doing, and will do during the monitoring stage of the project.

Chapter 12: Benefits of Project Management Tools

After getting to know about the importance of the monitoring stage of project completion, let's move on to certain management tools you should know about, and the benefits using such tools can offer.

To see how a project's progress is going, there are certain goals and milestones which need to achieved. Of course, there are a number of tasks you need to complete to reach each milestone. Using project management tools can help make everything streamlined.

So, what is a project management software or PM software?

As the name implies, PM software is software which is used to help you with managing a project, whether it is a big project or a small one.

As mentioned already, project management involves the process of planning, executing, monitoring, and ensuring the project is able to be completed at an appropriate time.

For you to go about effectively with all these things, there are resources, tools, skills, and techniques which need to be used.

Breaking these down, and relating them to the benefits offered by a PM software, you need to keep in mind the:

1. **Scope:** In simple terms, this is how you define the size of the project by looking at its goals and the resources you will need. If the scope of a project changes, everything else is likely to be impacted.
2. **Resources:** This includes the people working on the project, the materials that are required, and the equipment you need. Also, the people working on the project need to have the skills to meet the demands of the project. Coming to the budget, are there any funds stored in case something goes wrong?
3. **Time:** This is all about time management. As a project manager, you should know how much time is required for the completion of certain tasks. Is there any time flexibility or everything needs to

be done on time to achieve success? What can you do if an issue arises? Can you make up for the time that's lost? There are a lot of questions project managers have to ask themselves.

Due to project management being complex, as the manager, you need to ensure having a streamlined system which works for everyone. This is where project management software comes in. Such kind of software have been developed to help you streamline the process, from the planning phase to the execution phase, the monitoring, and so on.

I don't know about you all, but because of the conversations I tend to have due to the circles I'm a part of, I have noticed that project managers who don't use PM software are likely to end up facing certain issues.

These issues include spending more time than necessary on certain tasks, wasting more money than necessary on certain tasks, repetition of tasks, miscommunication, and more. Of course, the likelihood of experiencing such issues also depend on the size of a project.

You might have been able to meet your goals while working on a project that only has four people without using a PM software.

But ask yourself, do you think you would be able to manage everything if you are working with larger teams? Even teams that happen to be in a different geographical location than yours? Don't you think it would be better if you have a PM software to make things easier for you as a project manager?

The benefits a good PM software can offer are:

1. **Collaboration**

There can be many people working on the same project, with everyone having their specific tasks to take care of inside a team. A PM software can aid in improving overall collaboration inside a team as well as between teams.

For example, by using a PM software, a member of the team can keep the rest of the members updated about what they are working on. Furthermore, if an issue arises, they can use the PM software to contact the appropriate person in the team to handle the situation.

Also, as the project manager, you can monitor all of this by using the same software and look at the progress in real-time. You can also jump in when required and communicate with the team as a whole instead of remembering to send emails to everyone.

When it comes to improving collaboration, PM software offer:

- **File Sharing:** Files can be shared quickly with everyone using such software as long as the members have been granted access to the said software and its contents. You can add images, graphs, and more depending on the kind of information that's required.
- **Team communication:** Certain PM software come with their own messaging system which enables teams to stay in contact with each other and having a record of the conversations as well.

2. **Scheduling**

Without any type of system to be used, it can be tough for teams to keep on track when working on a project. Having a set schedule or plan acts as a guideline or timeframe for others to follow, giving them a sense of what needs to be done and when it needs to be done. It also lets them know who needs to handle what.

Being unclear about schedules lead to unproductivity, and as a project manager, you don't want that, right?

Of course, having sticky notes posted on a board along with printouts of schedules can help. But why surround yourself with all such clutter?

Using a PM software can help with scheduling everything on a virtual plane. You can make the deadlines clear, how the tasks should be prioritized, and more. Furthermore, editing certain things, if and when necessary, becomes easier when you are using a software and everyone concerned is instantly alerted about the edits made.

A PM software can help with:

- **Prioritizing:** As mentioned, through such a software you can easily prioritize tasks and let everyone know about it. Also, if due to certain changes a task needs to be fast-tracked the team can be easily notified about such a change.

- **Calendar:** Certain software have calendars which you can use to highlight important dates. This includes deadlines, the milestones that need to be reached during a set week, when something needs to be checked when meetings are going to be held. When the entire team has a calendar they can follow, communication and collaboration is increased.

- **Time worked:** PM software can also help you keep an eye on the amount of time a certain team member has worked on their task. Knowing the speed with which someone has been working on something allows you, as the project manager, to decide if that certain someone needs to be given more work or perhaps a one-on-one meeting because they need to pick up speed if they wish to meet the upcoming deadline.

3. **Managing Resource**

Considering the size of a project, there are many resources you will need to keep an eye on. Having a PM software can help you record the total budget you have, the amount which has been used, the team that used it up, and more. You can also keep a list of the materials you require and if more things need to be added. A software can help prevent you from overusing resources or not realizing the lack of them as the project progresses.

You might think a simple Excel sheet can help you out with everything. And you know what? It might have been working quite well for you in the past. But then again, ask yourself, will be able to cut it when you are assigned as the project manager of a very expensive project with many teams under you?

- **Reports:** Certain PM software are capable of providing you daily, weekly, and even monthly budget reports complete with graphs and all that visual flair to make things easier to keep track of. You can also share them with other team members.

- **Invoicing:** You can use PM software to keep track of pending or upcoming invoices with just a few clicks.

4. **Documentation**

Proper documentation is vital if you wish to ensure everything is on track and information is being stored for future use.

A PM software gives you:

- **Centralized storage:** Depending on who has access, team members can go ahead and store invoices, completed tasks, planned tasks, and everything else in a centralized storage system. Others, and even you can look at the documents you require without having to waste time finding certain folders or emails. Furthermore, using PM software to store data allows you to have a backup copy of everything, which can come in handy if the device you stored data on is damaged, lost or you don't have it near when you need to handle something urgent.

While the benefits of a PM software are there, determining if you need to use one is essential, too.

You should consider opting for a PM software if you don't want to encounter certain issues such as:

- Delaying of a project due to long email chains which lead to important data being buried.
- Confusing spreadsheets.
- Being unclear about approaching deadlines.
- Being unclear about who is supposed to handle what task.
- Poor communication between team members.
- Not having well-detailed status reports.
- Overlapping of work.
- Repetition of work.

- Not being clear about milestones that need to be met.
- Poor monitoring of a project's progress.
- Unclear scheduling

When it comes to selecting a PM software, you need consider the things pertaining to your project. Not every PM software is the same, and thus, some of them might not be able to give you what you want.

So, do your research and narrow down the options to a PM software which caters to all your needs. You might need to use two PM software to handle the kind of work you have, but personally, I wouldn't recommend any more than that. You shouldn't let the project software you're using become a hindrance to the project's progress.

Also, don't hesitate to take some time and demo the options you have. Many PM software offer free trials. Use them and see what works best for you and the team.

Chapter 13: Selecting the Right Project Management Style

Understanding Project Management Styles

To be an efficient project manager, you need to know about the project management style which needs to be used. The style you will use will depend a lot on the type of project you're working on.

So, let's go over the different types of project management styles that exist and which can be the perfect fit for the type of project you find yourself handling.

1. **Traditional Style**

Many of you might already be familiar with the traditional style of project management. This is where you come up with an idea, do your research and plan how to achieve the end goal, head on to the execution phase, the monitoring phase, and see it to completion.

You have a system in place when you follow the stages involved in such project management. You know you need to begin with an idea and then take it from there. For example, you wish to create a website. You have an idea about the type of website you want. You work on designing the logo, the layout, the type of content it will have, and then make the website live.

Similar stuff when you're creating an app. You have done your research, and you have an idea about what you the app to be for. You gather a team of coders, the design team, the testers, and so on, and you enter the execution stage, monitor the process, and then publish the app.

2. **Waterfall Style**

You will see that this one is similar to the traditional style of project management. As the name implies, this is a very linear approach of managing a project, like a waterfall, things are moving in a fixed way. Expanding on that, in this type of style, the members of a team are dependent on the completion of certain tasks before their own can reach completion. This type of style is recommended when you are working with a large team, and you require effective communication between everyone.

This style is also suitable when the project has to be done in a strict manner. What I mean by this is, for example, you are working on creating a new product, and you are working with many teams. The product is such one team can't move forward with their work unless another team has done theirs.

For example, you can't begin packaging a project until it has been produced. So, you are making a bar of soap. You know what kind of soap you want, how it will look, and all that stuff. The first thing for you to do will be to manage the manufacturing process. Once that's done, the soap will be sent out for packaging, and that's when the packaging team will come in, ready to pack it all up and have it ready for launch. So, it is a very systematic way of doing things where a certain team's work is dependent on another's.

Let's go for another example about app creation. The said app need to have certain features. You talk to the client about the features and what can be achieved and what can't so you're both on the same page of understanding. This constitutes the Requirement phase.

So, you go ahead and begin developing the said app. This is the Development phase. The testing phase also helps to identify certain bugs or things that need to be changed. You keep working on this phase until you have a product the client is happy with and that's the Acceptance phase at which point you are done.

Of course, there are teams who tend to do things differently when using the waterfall style.

A disadvantage of this style is it doesn't allow a lot of room for changes. If something needs to be changed, you might need to start from scratch.

3. **Agile Style**

In this style of project management, the sequence of the tasks that need to be done are broken down into milestones. This also means it becomes easier for you to add changes when necessary, allowing you to adapt upcoming tasks in a manner that works for everyone and aids in keeping the project on the right path. Such an approach allows you to keep in communication with the team.

Such a style has also been followed by a range of companies. Including big ones like IBM, mid-sized and even startups.

This style can work for projects that don't have strict final requirements. What I mean by this is while you know what kind of result you want, there is room for some changes. Such a style, through the experience I've had, seems to work well with releasing app updates or website updates.

You know what main features an app update needs to have. There is also a list of secondary features that need to be released. With this style, everything is done in increments and released when the task is completed without their being a delay in the overall project.

The only thing you need to keep in mind when using this style is keeping the scope in style. When there aren't a lot of strictness pertaining to the final goals of a project, the scope can change. Furthermore, with there being changes that need to be made, you have to make sure everything is communicated properly.

Also, keep an eye on the documentation, including data related to the updates or changes. Keep in mind this style might not be the best when working on a project that has strict deadlines.

Let's go over an example. Think you're working on someone's hair as a stylist. If you were working with the waterfall style, you would go in a systematic approach after gathering all of the information about what the style needs to be. In the Agile approach, you will go in a manner that continues to take the client's feedback, making changes whenever required to deliver the result. You allow the client to make changes as you continue.

Furthermore, this is also a style which has been used in app development or even when writing a book or designing a house. You keep the client in the loop and make certain changes, relating with what the client wants, as you go toward completing a project.

4. **Strategic Style**

In the strategic project management style, you have to have in mind the big picture of what needs to be done. You need to come up with a strategy to meet the expectations of the organization in an efficient manner. This is about anticipating issues that might arise and being ready to solve them. This style also involves opting for more focused hires. Basically, it is about making plans for the future while keeping in mind the core values of an organization.

Such type of management can be used when introducing something new to the organization, even if it is just changes to make the workplace a better environment for everyone.

5. **Scrum Style**

This is defined as regular meet-ups of concerned team members to discuss the project's status, results, updates, and similar data. You can tell this style is about forming strong communication between the teams working on a project. This style can work for you when everyone is dependent on each other to complete tasks. This is also a good style when working on innovations and you require constant input from the team you are managing.

A good time to use such a style is when you are working on large projects which has a lot of things that need to be accomplished. However, due to this style requiring communication from all involved teams, it won't do you any good if the teams aren't motivated to share useful data, feedback or miss the scheduled meeting times.

While these are five project management styles you should know about, also keep in mind project management is evolving and will continue evolving due to the changing business landscape. There is a lot of strategy involved. That is why, if you want my opinion, I recommend not sticking to one specific style. Look at the demands of an organization and then use a combination of different styles (if necessary) to achieve the project's goals.

Why put yourself in a box as a project manager, right? Being able to adapt to changes and pivoting a project when necessary are skills many organizations want PMs to possess.

Just remember not to go overboard. Changing styles on a whim can confuse the teams you're working with.

The Correct Project Management Style for You

As a project manager, you should know about your own project management style. Also, the good news is you can change up your styles depending on the scope of the project or the kind of teams you are working with.

Everyone approaches job in their own manner. With experience, you will get to understand what works best for you and how you can mold certain things to accommodate any type of project you're working on. Also, the organization might ask you about your project management style during the interview process. I will talk about picking up becoming a project manager as a viable career as this course continues.

So, the project manager styles are:

1. **Authoritative**

Such project managers naturally draw respect from the teams they're dealing with. They have authoritative air about them. However, they are open to listening to others and know how to deal with issues in an appropriate manner.

2. **Democratic**

Such managers involve others in the entire process. They are good with empowering others by recognizing the strengths of each individual and making them feel motivated about the work they are being asked to do. A project manager with a democratic style also listens to experts in the fields. Such a manager trusts the team and gives them more freedom with how they manage a task.

3. **Coercive**

Project managers who are coercive tend to be quite strict. You might see this style being used when inexperienced teams are being handled. Due to the project manager knowing what is required, they are strict with the involved teams who might not be very clear about what's expected of them. There isn't much freedom given to teams in this style.

4. **Pace-Setter**

These project managers are more focused on getting the work quickly done because of strict deadlines. They don't offer a lot of freedom to the teams. This style can help when managing project that are simpler but need to done quite quickly. For example, after getting a certain amount of customer feedback, a new update for an app needs to be rolled out. The work is simple, and the project manager, using this style will set the pace to ensure the update is done as quickly as possible. Such a style also works when managing a small team.

5. **Affiliative**

These are the kind of project managers who, after giving clear instructions, tend to check in once in a while. They allow teams to work in the manner they want as long as the deadlines are being met. You will see this kind of management style if the project is being handled by an experienced team. The project manager trusts the team and simply links everyone together while the teams work on completing the project.

So, what's best for you?

As I've already mentioned, there's no need for you to put yourself in a box and constrict yourself. Don't hesitate to change up your managing styles to accommodate the type of project you're working on.

However, changing up styles every day isn't going to help you or the project. You need to decide on the style or the combination of styles you will be using during the planning phase. You might have authoritative air about you, but still, have some level of a democratic approach. Again, it all depends on the scope of the project and the type of teams you're working with.

For example, if you're working with an experienced team, you can't handle the said team in the manner you would manage newbies who are still trying to figure out how to do correctly handle the tasks they're given.

Don't be afraid to evolve.

Chapter 14: How Do You Become a Project Manager?

Becoming a project manager can be a very lucrative career for you if you are passionate about such a field.

If you are wondering about how much you can make as a project manager, well, according to the stats from Glassdoor, the average base pay for a project manager in the United States is around $90,300 a year.

It is around $59,000 at the lower end with up to $130,000 at the higher end. It all depends on your experience and the field you work in as a project manager.

For those wondering about working as a freelance project manager, according to data from ZipRecruiter, the average pay for a freelance project manager in the US is $78,800 a year. The higher end is $148,000 with the lower being $21,000 on average. Again, it all depends on the experience you have and the type of project you're working on.

If you wish to become a project manager, but you don't know where to start, let me help you out.

The first thing you need to do is research about what it means to become a project manager. I have done what I'm able to help you out with this through this book. You should understand what is meant by a project manager and the responsibilities they have. You should look at the skills a project manager should possess.

Don't hesitate to read about what other project managers have done and how you their journey can help yours. If possible, get in contact with other project managers. Having a good mentor can aid in your reaching the heights of success you wish for.

Also, looking for certain degrees and certificates you which can help you as a project manager is important, too. You should also read up on different project management tools available. Opting for an internship can help you, too. Make use of platforms such as Udemy to find project manager courses capable of offering you some valuable knowledge.

Also, ask yourself... are you someone who is a leader and can manage entire projects from the planning phase all the way to completion? If you think you can, then yes, by all means, continue on your journey.

Project Manager Education

Some of you might be wondering about any educational pre-requisites you need to have to become an accomplished project manager. Well, you can begin by working to get a project manager or a business administration degree. However, even if you don't have a degree, it doesn't mean you are at a disadvantage.

The good news is being a project manager isn't exclusive to a particular field. You can become a project manager in the field of art, IT, business, software, economics, and more. Organizations in every field are looking to hire capable project managers. It all depends on the kind of field you wish to work in. So, see what degree you already have and how they can help with pursue the project manager career you want.

For example, an app development house might be looking for someone with a software or an app developer degree because they want to hire a person who understands the field better.

Furthermore, you can work your way up to the position of a project manager by starting small. You can opt for an internship. You can begin as a project manager assistant on a small project. Gaining such valuable experience will train you to be ready for the type of work you will handle as a professional project manager down the line.

As for project management certifications, you should consider picking them up. As you work yourself up the ladder in your progress, you might feel the need to get certain certifications. Even an organization might want you to get a certification before they can consider you for a promotion. You might not feel them to very valuable, and frankly, they might not be. However, the experience you will be able to collect through the training sessions you will go through to get certified will help you in the long run.

And besides, having all the degrees, diplomas and certificates aren't going to be any use to you if you haven't gained experience which can help you handle actual projects. So, take your time and see which route is better for you to gain the knowledge you need.

If you're wondering about certifications, you should go for the:

1. **PMP certification**

This stands for the Project Management Professional certification which is offered by PMI or the Project Management Institute. This type of certification is something organizations accept because not everyone can go ahead and sit for the test.

For those who don't know, it consists of 200 multiple-choice questions. It also requires the person to have at least three years of working experience as a project manager. A total of 5 years is a minimum if the person doesn't have a PM degree. There is also 35 hours of formal education on project management along with a minimum of 4,500 hours of experience related to directing a project. If you don't have a four-year degree, the hours go up to 7,500.

The PMP certification is deemed valuable in Canada, the U.S, and the Middle East. For those in Europe, or wanting to work in Europe, you can opt for the PRINCE2 certification.

2. **CAPM Certification**

If you can't take the PMP exam at this time, you can opt for the Certified Associate in Project Management examination or the CAPM certification. Such a certification will let organizations know you are serious about pursuing becoming a PM.

3. **PRINCE2 Certification**

This stands for PRojects IN Controlled Environments. I know it feels like they really wanted the abbreviation to be PRINCE. This is a good one to have if you wish to work in the UK or other parts of Europe.

The learning paths include:

- **PRINCE2 Foundation**

This is the first level which confirms the basic knowledge you have regarding this method. While there are no prerequisites for you to worry about, you should have project management experience.

- **PRINCE2 Practitioner**

Through this level you get the confirmation you know how to use the PRINCE2 method in the real world. This is what will let organizations know you can be a good candidate for employment if they are looking for someone who can bring the PRINCE2 method's principles the project that needs to be worked on.

Chapter 15: Freelancing or a Traditional Hire as a Project Manager?

Freelancing as a Project Manager

Let's talk about freelancing as a project manager. Depending on your expertise and the kind of projects you handle, you can make a nice amount of money in your career. As a project manager, you can make anywhere from $100 to even $50,000 or more. It all depends on how you present yourself and the connections you are able to make.

As a freelance project manager you might be asked by a client to work on:

- Improving a security application
- To help create or launch a blog
- Create a logo
- To set up online stores
- Manage or build the backend of a website
- Improve customer service
- And more

Now, if you plan on working as a freelance project manager, you need to know certain logistics as well to ensure you are able to create a career without hassle.

To set up your business as a freelance Project Manager, the logistics are:

1. It is recommended that you create a brand for yourself as a project manager.

2. You will need to purchase the raw material (equipment and software) to start running your business as a freelance project manager. This might include certain project monitoring software, a laptop or computer, and such.

Some other things, if you are working as a freelancer, include:

- **Website**

As a freelance project manager, you should consider having a website for yourself. Like I said, as a freelancer, you need to work on your brand. Having a website helps to add value to your freelance work and even reaches to out potential customers. You can use the website to display your work, the things you have created or the projects you have worked on for others. Your degrees and certifications as well. Think of your website as a portfolio which you can use to get your name out there. Furthermore, through your website, you can also maintain a blog section and interact with the community by offering tips about Project management or maybe write about your journey as a project manager.

- **Market**

As a freelance project manager, it is very important you know how to market yourself. This is something that people being traditionally hired don't have to worry about. However, you, as a freelancer, will need to promote yourself to get potential clients. Again, having a website can help you market yourself and create an online presence for your brand. Networking is going to be important for you as a freelancer. So, don't hesitate to build new connections in the Project manager community to help your career.

- **Staying Up-to-Date**

Be ready to learn new things. Keep an eye on different project management tools that are being introduced. See what projects organizations are working on. Go for new certifications that can help improve your brand as a project manager. You don't want to lose a potential client just because you didn't know how to use the latest version of a certain tool.

Working on Your Project Manager Resume

If you mean to be hired as project manager by an organization, you need to make sure you have an impressive resume. From my experience, many capable project managers weren't hired for a job because their resume didn't look great. I know it might sound weird, but that's how the world works. You are going to be judged on your resume, and that's why you need to make sure it can stand out from the rest.

When there is a job opening you're interested in, always make sure to read the details. Look at the role and responsibilities of the person who will be hired. Make sure you read the requirements. These include proper experience, any trainings the person should have gone through, the skills that an organization are looking for as well as any certifications which are preferred.

So, when you are ready to submit your resume, make sure it has the information that matches with what's written on the job opening. Provide information about the How, When, and Where you did everything. Don't hesitate to show where you had similar roles and responsibilities and how that experience can help the organization which is interested in hiring.

Keep in mind to:

- Make it easy for the reviewer to read your resume. Do not add in information they aren't looking or asking for.
- Have your resume updated on your LinkedIn profile.
- Make it clear how your experience can help an organization with their need.
- Be short and concise.
- Offer data about projects you have worked for, the scope you handled, and the result.
- Let them know about the project budgets you have handled.
- Add any awards you received as well as the awards the project, which you worked on a project manager, received.
- Talk about the tools you are capable of using.
- Have a second pair of eyes on the resume and see if they can offer you some constructive criticism.

FAQs – Freelancing as a Project Manager

As a freelance project manager, you are likely going to have certain questions about how the business side of things are going to go. I hope the answers I have provided give you the information you have been looking for in this regard.

- **How do you market your services as a freelance project manager?**

Again, like I said, it all comes down to how much you are able to promote yourself and network. Having a website is going to help you with this. Furthermore, networking and creating connections inside the project manager community can also give you leads for potential clients.

Once you reach out to a client, or they contact you, it is important that you know what to bring to the table. Be transparent about the kind of projects you can handle. Your proposal should let your client know what they will be paying you for. Also, leaving a good impression on your client, even if it isn't the biggest of projects, can help strengthen your reputation in the field and lead to more jobs.

- **Is there a list of websites I can use to look for jobs?**

Of course, there is such a list of websites you can use to look for jobs. The websites include:

- Crew
- Indeed
- Devcenter
- Upwork
- Freelancer
- Truelance
- Fiverr
- Creative Staffing Agency

Yes, there are many more websites for you to use to help procure a job for yourself. It all depends on what works for you and your level of expertise as a project manager.

- **Where can you sell your services as a freelance project manager?**

There are many ways for you to sell your skills in project manager and get paid for them. As a freelancer, going to related conventions can help you network and search out job openings. You can also signup for certifications and make connections through there. There are companies (mostly small ones) looking for freelance work, and they are more than willing to pay you by the hour if that's what you prefer.

Also, again, your website is going to act as a portfolio and perhaps the biggest platform which you can use to not only promote your work but also sell your services to interested clients.

Working with a Traditional Business as a Project Manager

If you wish to work as a traditional business hire, the job requirements are going to be more or less the same as a freelancer project manager. This means that the set of skills you will need are likely going to be similar. Working with a company, the job description is going to change depending on what you are working on as well as the company you work for.

Working as a Project Manager for a company can bring with itself a lot of benefits for you. As a company hire, you might be invited to many corporate events. You might even be asked to travel the world, attending certain conventions, going for certifications, health benefits, and more.

Using Social Media to Find Jobs as a Project Manager

While I have talked about the ways you can market yourself as a project manager, using your website and networking, you can also reach out to potential clients through social media. The three social media platforms you should use to help build your career are:

1. **LinkedIn**

LinkedIn is meant for professional networking, and you need to use it for that, especially if you want to start as a freelancer. It serves as a platform that connects potential employers with potential employees and vice versa. You can create an account if you do not have one already, set up your profile and start looking for prospective employers that are interested in hiring a project manager.

You will need to do your research to find potential job opportunities. Also, remember employers too can see your profile and if they like what they see, they will contact you themselves. So, make sure to improve your profile as much as you can. LinkedIn allows you to add updates which can help you share with others what you have been working on.

2. **Facebook**

Facebook is another extremely popular social media platform, being able to connect people from all over the world. From a business perspective, you may join groups that are related to employment for project managers. Many businesses also have Facebook pages where they post about any job openings they might have. So, keeping an eye on such pages can help you find a job for yourself.

You can also make a Facebook page for yourself where you can post updates about the new projects you are working on, your rates as a project manager, etc. Now, even if Facebook doesn't seem to be the best option for you right now, it doesn't hurt to try.

3. **Twitter**

Twitter is a great way for you to network not only with relevant companies in your field but also with other project management enthusiasts. Some companies do tweet about potential job openings. Furthermore, it is a great way for you to build an online presence for yourself by tweeting about articles you might like, what you are working on, replying to other enthusiasts, and such.

I mentioned social media in this course because the important thing for you to do is network if you wish to make a career out of the project management skills you have. Networking and building connections is extremely important if you happen to be finding a job as a freelance project manager. You should also consider joining project manager forums for networking purposes.

Freelancing or a Regular Hire as a Project Manager?

Although this career path is long, I have tried to share all the important aspects that should be considered for a career as a project manager. Choosing to work as a freelance or with a company as a Project Manager completely depends upon you.

Just bear in mind the fact that no option is wrong. One individual may choose freelancing because they may be suited for that type of work. Every person will have different capabilities. So, select a route you are comfortable with.

My conclusive advice to all of you out there would be to carefully weigh the pros and cons of both paths. You may even consult your family and friends and make the decision that will make you happy.

As mentioned in this course, there is financial gain in both the options. Organizations are going to continue requiring project managers so you will continue having opportunities come your way if you're a capable project manager.

It all depends on you.

So, choose wisely!

Chapter 16: Bonus - The Difference Between Leadership and Management

Before I bring this book to a close, I would like to take a few minutes to talk about the difference between leadership and management.

There are people out there who confuse leadership and management. You should know they aren't the same thing. The main difference is that leaders are one whom people follow while managers are someone who have others working for them.

Leadership is about getting people involved after they understand the vision you have. A leader's job is to make people believe in the goals of an organization. Management deals more with administering the process and monitoring daily activities and ensuring everything is working in an appropriate manner.

As a project manager, you should work on being both the leader and manager. While they aren't the same thing, they are linked. For a project to be completed in a successful manner, you, as the project manager, along with offering management that plans and knows how to coordinate need to inspire and motive teams as a leader would.

Efficient project managers look at people as more than skilled workforce. They work in inspiring and motivating them to get the best results possible. Such project managers know a motivated team is capable of achieving a lot.

So, don't think you need to keep others at bay when you become a project manager, only giving instructions and expecting the work to be done. As mentioned in this book, a good project manager is also a good listener. They know how to keep others motivated. They stay in communication with the teams they're working with and are ready to address any issues they might have. Such project managers understand the importance of making others feel invested in what they're doing.

A balance between management and leadership is required. Of course, you need to do your project manager duties, ensuring everyone is keeping up with the schedule, doing the work that's needed, and such, but you can also do what you can to inspire teams and allow them to feel that they are needed and well-respected when it comes to the project they're handling.

Chapter 17: Summary and Conclusion

Thank you so much for keeping up with me throughout this Project Management book. I hope I was able to offer you all of the information you required to make a decision about whether or not you should opt for such a career path and how you can improve yourself as a project manager.

As mentioned, more than 90% of organizations are in search for a capable project manager, and they will continue looking for capable professionals to make a projects a success. Proper project management is the key to the success of any project. There's the planning phase, the execution phase, the monitoring, and taking the project all the way to completion. As a project manager, you will need to be a leader as well as a manager. You will need to know about the proper ways to communicate and ensure the team you're working with has an environment that promotes collaboration to bring forth the best results.

Furthermore, as far as freelancing and traditional hire opportunities go, both routes can offer you very lucrative careers as a project manager.

So, again, it all comes down to what you wish to achieve in your professional life.

Again, I thank you for selecting this course. And good luck for what you decide to do as a project manager.

Please feel free to tell others about this book so they too can benefit from the information I have shared.

Thank you!

www.ingramcontent.com/pod-product-compliance
Lightning Source LLC
Chambersburg PA
CBHW030704220526
45463CB00005B/1901